famous
friends of the
wolf
cook book

famous friends of the wolf cookbook

benefiting wolf recovery in the west

Nancy Reid & Sheila Liermann

featuring photographs by Jim Dutcher and Jim Brandenburg

Adams Media Corporation

Holbrook, Massachusetts

Published by
Adams Media Corporation
260 Center Street, Holbrook, MA 02343

ISBN: 1-55850-632-2

Printed in Canada.

J I H G F E D C B A

Reid, Nancy.
Famous friends of the wolf cookbook; benefiting wolf recovery in the West/Nancy Reid & Sheila Liermann.
p. cm.
Includes index.
ISBN 1-55850-632-2 (hardcover)
1. Cookery, International. 2. Celebrities—West (U.S.) 3. Wolves—West (U.S.) I. Liermann, Sheila K. II. Title.
TX725.A1R447 1996
641.59—dc20   96-17247
                                                                                       CIP

Grateful acknowledgment is made to the following for permission to reprint material:

From *The Ninemile Wolves* by Rick Bass. Copyright © 1992 Rick Bass. Ballantine Books, Inc. Reprinted by permission of the author.

From *Brother Wolf* by Jim Brandenburg. Copyright © 1993 Jim Brandenburg. NorthWord Press, Inc. Reprinted by permission of the author.

From Notes for *Women Who Run With the Wolves* by Clarissa Pinkola Estés, Ph.D. Copyright © 1971, 1979, 1992 Clarissa Pinkola Estés, Ph.D. Reprinted by permission of the author.

Hungarian Goulash from Marushka Pinkola by Clarissa Pinkola Estés, Ph.D. Copyright © 1994 Clarissa Pinkola Estés, Ph.D. Reprinted by permission of the author.

From *A Sand County Almanac, with Other Essays on Conservation from Round River* by Aldo Leopold. Copyright © 1949, 1953, 1966, renewed 1977, 1981 Oxford University Press, Inc. Reprinted by permission of Oxford University Press.

From *Of Wolves and Men* by Barry Holstun Lopez. Copyright © 1978 Barry Holstun Lopez. Charles Scribner's Sons, a division of Macmillan Publishing Company. Reprinted by permission of the author.

From *Linda McCartney's Home Cooking* by Linda McCartney. Copyright © 1989 MPL Communications Ltd. Arcade Publishing, Inc., a Little, Brown Company. Reprinted by permission of the author.

From *Chez Panisse Pasta, Pizza and Calzone Cookbook* by Alice L. Waters. Copyright © 1984 Random House, Inc. Reprinted by permission of the author.

Hummus (Chickpea Sauce) with Shrimp, from Rockpool Restaurant, Sydney Australia. Copyright © 1993 Acorn Associates, Ltd. Reprinted by permission of Burt Wolf.

Madam Wazell's Roadhouse Steak by Texas Bix Bender. Copyright © 1994 Texas Bix Bender. Reprinted by permission of the author

Cover photos: Yellow Wolf, Warrior, Nez Perce Tribe (©Montana Historical Society, Helena, Montana), Candice Bergen, Andie MacDowell, Robert Redford, Ted Turner (©George Bennett), Jane Fonda, Wolves (©Jim Dutcher)

Book and cover design by E Design, Eloise Christensen and Penfield Stroh.
Illustrations and sketches throughout the text and journal © Lori McNee Watson.
Calligraphy by Wendy Watson and wolf silhouettes by Pat Feldman Hoffman.

This book is available at quantity discounts for bulk purchases.
For information, call 1-800-872-5627 (in Massachusetts, 617-767-8100).

Visit our home page at http://www.adamsmedia.com

from the wolf education and research center

Between 1600 and 1930, man annihilated almost every wolf pack in the United States—an estimated two million wolves. Old World tales such as *Little Red Riding Hood* reinforced myths about the nature of the wolf and, for many, justified the slaughter of this noble and misunderstood animal.

Many famous friends of the wolf, from astronaut Buzz Aldrin to Richard and Lili Fini Zanuck, have generously donated their time and their favorite recipes for this cookbook in an effort to undo this ugly past and return the wolf to its natural habitat. Our thanks to all of them.

Bringing the gray wolf back to the Northern Rockies is a complicated and costly undertaking. In 1995, the U.S. Fish and Wildlife Service began capturing a few wild wolves in Canada and releasing them in central Idaho and Yellowstone National Park. Biologists expect that a target population of 100 wolves will be reached by the year 2002 in each of these areas.

A portion of the royalties generated by this cookbook will be donated to the Wolf Recovery Action Fund, a Wolf Education and Research Center program designed to help offset the cost of wolf recovery in the Northern Rockies. In a unique partnership, the Fund offers financial assistance to public agencies, universities, and organizations that are leading the charge.

The money is used to directly benefit recovery: buying radio collars to monitor released wolves, educating ranchers on how to minimize depredation, enhancing habitat to increase prey populations, and financing other critical needs.

The Wolf Education and Research Center is a nonprofit group headquartered in Boise, Idaho. In 1996, WERC established a wolf center on Nez Perce tribal land near Winchester, Idaho. The Center will feature exhibits on wolves and related endangered species, Native American culture, and a 20-acre natural habitat enclosure for the Sawtooth Pack—captive-born wolves that serve as ambassadors for their wild relatives.

While people are not usually introduced to an endangered species in the kitchen, we think this is a great opportunity to tell the wolf's story in a delectable manner. We hope that you will better understand this spirited animal after reading *Famous Friends of the Wolf.*

Enjoy.

For Wolves,

Diana Hewett
President

Suzanne Laverty
Program Director

It is not by accident

that over the eons the wolf is one of the most common animals that human beings dream about. When some basic thread of a human being's life has broken or become unraveled, the spirit of the wolf often shows up in night dreams. Healthy wolves and healthy humans share certain psychic characteristics: keen sensing, playful spirit, and a heightened capacity for devotion. Wolves are relational by nature, inquiring, possessed of great endurance and strength. They are deeply intuitive, intensely concerned with their young, their mate and their pack. They are experienced in adapting to constantly changing circumstances, they are fiercely stalwart and very brave. The wolf's appearance in a person's dream may be a reference to the integrity of living in cycles, a directive regarding the repair of injured instincts, or a reminder of one's innate strength, and knowing.

Psychoanalytically, it is not untoward to conclude, that if in reality the species known as wolf were truly eradicated by humans, that its significant influence as a predictive and life-inspiring image in the symbolic language of dreams would be eradicated also.

One of the matters given no notice in discussions about the wolf—or any other of nature's creatures for that matter—is this critical psychic fact: When we eradicate living creatures from our outer environs, within a few generations they become desaparecidos, *they are massacred in the dream world as well.*

—Clarissa Pinkola Estés, Ph.D.
from Notes for *Women Who Run With the Wolves*

contents
wolves

cooks

© Jim Brandenburg

preface

For nearly two million years, wolves flourished and scattered across the northern half of the earth. They hunted, played, and howled in forests, prairies, and deserts, on steppes, tundra, and ice fields, adapting to virtually every habitat and climate. Once the most widely distributed land mammal in the world, the species is now extinct, or nearly so, over most of its historic range.

The world's largest concentration of wolves, an estimated 100,000, is believed to exist in the former Soviet Union. In North America, the wolf is tenaciously hanging on to the northernmost, and less inhabited, reaches of its original range. There are an estimated 50,000 in Canada and another 6,000 in Alaska. The largest population of wolves in the Lower 48 states, about 2,000, is in northeastern Minnesota and Isle Royale in Lake Superior.

Wolves are showing up in Montana, trickling down from Canada. The new immigrants have carved out a handful of home territories in the Big Sky state, and after decades of relentless persecution, they are making a slow comeback.

Jim Dutcher

Wolves are making a comeback of a different nature in Idaho and Yellowstone National Park. On the endangered species list since 1973, the gray wolf is once again howling in these wild areas. In a historical turnabout, wolves have been arriving in the arms of biologists. Beginning in early 1995, wild wolves were captured in Canada by wildlife biologists, and then released in the nation's first national park and in Idaho's vast wilderness. U.S. Fish and Wildlife Service biologists will closely monitor the transplants' progress until 100-some wolves roam in each of the areas and the wolf is deemed "fully recovered."

We live in the small town of Ketchum, near the wolf's range in central Idaho. If the transplanted wolves gain a foothold, the chances of hearing a pack howl on a camping trip or a backcountry ski may be better than the chances of finding a parking place in New York City. That wild possibility has fueled our interest in wolves and our enthusiasm for this book. We know our lives will be enriched by wild wolves.

The people you will read about in this cookbook—actors, Olympians, authors, artists, environmentalists, biologists, and other recipe contributors—all share the goal of returning the wolf to his historic ranges in the Northern Rockies. Toward this goal, they have shared part of their lives—their food traditions. Some of the recipes are family favorites passed down from one pack to another. Many are savory dishes cooked over and over again because they fit busy lifestyles and taste wonderful every time. A few of the recipes are entertaining stories about how food transects life. Cook from this book, read it, laugh, and join in the howling camaraderie. *Famous Friends of the Wolf Cookbook* holds the secret to a great repast.

Throughout the book you will see the spirit of the wolf through the camera lens of two of America's top wildlife photographers. Cinematographer Jim Dutcher produced and filmed *Water, Birth, the Planet Earth* and *Rocky Mountain Beaver Pond* for National Geographic. He went on to create two films for ABC's *World of Discovery, Cougar: Ghost of the Rockies* and *Wolf: Return of a Legend.* He received an Emmy for the latter.

Andrew Baugnet

Jim Brandenburg

Dutcher captured the essence of the wolf in his photos from Wolf Camp. Dutcher founded the camp and has introduced three sets of pups to the Sawtooth Wolf Camp and into the camp's 20-acre enclosure below the 10,000-foot peaks of Idaho's Sawtooth Mountains. The images he has caught on film have been critical in bringing the life of the pack into the homes and hearts of the American public.

Jim Brandenburg is one of a few to photograph wolves extensively in the wild. His images of Arctic wolves appeared in his book *White Wolf.* Later, in *Brother Wolf,* he captured the timber wolf in a collection of photos taken near Ravenwood, his home in northeastern Minnesota.

To accompany these stunning images, we have chosen some of our favorite passages, culled from what we think are the best of contemporary writings. We include the eloquent words of Rick Bass *(The Ninemile Wolves),* Aldo Leopold *(A Sand County Almanac, with Other Essays on Conservation from Round River),* Jim Brandenburg *(Brother Wolf),* Barry Holstun Lopez *(Of Wolves and Men),* and Clarissa Pinkola Estés *(*Notes for *Women Who Run With the Wolves).*

In creating this book, we wanted readers to experience face-to-face this wildest of animals; we wanted readers to run with wolves. We found that experience ourselves in a visit to Wolf Camp, and we knew that research biologist Megan Parker could take you on a foray with the pack, too. Initially, Megan served as our wolfe expert, a source for our many questions. During the time we researched this book, she lived at Wolf Camp, studying the captive-born Sawtooth Pack.

Sub-zero temperatures, a 130-pound alpha male, the yurt she called home 5 miles by snowshoe from the nearest road, the most brilliant set of stars on the planet, 60 miles to the nearest espresso machine, and no running water is Wolf Camp. Megan is one of the toughest women we have ever met. We became enchanted with her life and her stories about the pack, so we asked her to share her field notes. Her observations recorded at Wolf Camp are the basis of the Sawtooth Pack Journal.

We have learned a great deal about *Canis lupus* in the two years it took to put this book together. We have also learned a great deal about the people whom wolves attract. The biologists and advocates working to return the wolf to the wild can be as elusive as the shy predator. Yet, once a stranger is invited into the circle, its members are kind and helpful. Above all, these people are passionate about the wolf and it is that passion we hope to evoke here.

Lori McAfee Watson @'95

Buzz Aldrin

On July 20, 1969, an estimated 550 million people, the largest television audience ever, watched Buzz Aldrin and his partner, Neil Armstrong, take the first lunar steps. Back on Planet Earth, Aldrin continues to make great strides. He has designed a satellite space station, authored several books, and traveled the world teaching and learning about the latest ideas for exploring the universe. In his free time, Aldrin and his wife, Lois, support children's charities, dive the deep sea world, and ski the mountain tops of Sun Valley.

One-Step Pasta

A beautiful and sophisticated pasta dish, ideal for a special occasion or an intimate dinner with friends. It is divinely rich, yet the feta cheese and fresh herbs give it a sprightly accent.

1 pound large shrimp, peeled and deveined
$^1/_2$ teaspoon white pepper, or more to taste
2 tablespoons olive oil
3–5 cloves garlic, minced
5–6 stalks green onion, chopped into $^1/_2$-inch pieces
1 cup heavy cream
$1^1/_2$ cups chicken stock
$^3/_4$ cup dry vermouth
1 cup sun-dried tomatoes packed in oil, drained and slivered
3-ounce can tomato paste
1 pound linguine or spaghetti
1 cup feta cheese, crumbled
$^1/_4$ cup chopped fresh parsley
$^1/_4$ cup chopped fresh basil (or 1 tablespoon dried)

Sprinkle shrimp with white pepper, and let sit in the refrigerator for a few minutes. Heat oil in a large skillet. Sauté shrimp, garlic, and green onion over medium-high heat for 2–3 minutes. Transfer to a dish, cover, and set aside.

Reduce heat to medium. Using the same skillet, add cream, chicken stock, vermouth, sun-dried tomatoes, and tomato paste. Bring to a boil, reduce heat, and simmer on low until thickened, about 8 minutes. Return shrimp mixture to skillet. Cook only long enough to heat through, about 2–3 minutes.

Meanwhile, cook pasta according to package instructions. Drain well, and immediately toss with the sauce. Transfer to a large heated serving bowl, and sprinkle with feta cheese, parsley, and basil.

Serves 4–6

Spinach Frittata

Mike Bader submits this recipe from the field office of the Alliance for the Wild Rockies in Missoula, Montana, where he serves as executive director. He has also worked as a National Park Ranger in Yellowstone National Park, where he says he "wrestled grizzly bears, fought forest fires, and generally created havoc."

2 tablespoons vegetable oil
1 medium onion, finely chopped
2 packages frozen spinach (8 ounces each), thawed, or 1¹/₂ pounds fresh spinach,
well rinsed and chopped
5 eggs, beaten
1 pound shredded mozzarella cheese
salt and pepper to taste

Preheat oven to 325°. Butter the bottom and sides of a 2¹/₂-quart soufflé dish, and set aside.

Heat oil in a medium skillet. Sauté onion and spinach until excess moisture in the spinach has evaporated.

In a large bowl, combine eggs and cheese. Stir in spinach and onions, and mix well. Season to taste.

Pour mixture into prepared pan and spread evenly. Bake for about 35 minutes, or until frittata is puffy and cooked in the center. Cut into wedges and serve hot.

Serves 6

Alliance for the Wild Rockies

The Alliance for the Wild Rockies has set out to become the guardian angel of the Northern Rockies Ecosystem, the largest remaining tract of roadless wilderness and native forest in the Lower 48 states. Working through Congress and the courts, the grassroots group is seeking to protect this untouched land, which provides essential corridors linking animal and fish populations throughout the Northwest. The ecosystem—which includes parts of Washington, Oregon, Idaho, Montana, and Wyoming—still supports populations of every native mammal that lived when Lewis and Clark explored the area in 1804. Some of those species, however, are now threatened or endangered.

Edward Asner

Edward Asner divides his energy between dramatic projects and many political and charitable causes, including Defenders of Wildlife, Amnesty International, and the National Coalition to Abolish the Death Penalty. Asner narrated a television spot recently for Defenders that primed the nation for wolf reintroduction in Yellowstone. Accomplished in both comedy and drama, he was the grumpy boss, Lou Grant, with a big heart on *The Mary Tyler Moore Show* and later turned Lou Grant into its own series. Asner has won five Emmys for the character.

Edward Asner's Favorite Potatoes

This is a wonderful, lowfat dish that goes with anything. —E.A.

2 tablespoons olive oil
2 pounds small new potatoes, washed, patted dry, and quartered
1 tablespoon minced garlic
1 tablespoon minced shallot
1 teaspoon fresh thyme leaves, chopped
1 teaspoon finely chopped fresh rosemary
$1/8$ teaspoon freshly ground nutmeg
$1/4$ cup balsamic vinegar
salt and pepper to taste

Preheat oven to 400°.

Heat olive oil in a large skillet over medium-high heat. Add potatoes, garlic, and shallot, and toss together until well mixed. Sprinkle with thyme, rosemary, and nutmeg. Toss well. When potatoes are hot, transfer them to a baking sheet and spread in a single layer. (Recipe can be made several hours ahead to this point.)

Place baking sheet on rack in lower third of oven. Roast potatoes until golden and just tender, about 25 minutes, turning once midway. Remove from oven, drizzle vinegar over potatoes, and toss well. Season to taste with salt and pepper. Return to oven until sizzling, about 7 minutes. Serve immediately.

Serves 6

Edward Asner

Elwood Sandwich

This recipe is from Dan Aykroyd's House of Blues restaurant and club on Sunset Boulevard in Hollywood.

2 boneless, skinless chicken breasts (6 ounces each),
rinsed and patted dry
1 tablespoon butter or margarine
2 onion rolls
2 lettuce leaves
2 large tomato slices
3 tablespoons sour cream, divided
pickled jalapeño slices
Tabasco sauce

Louisiana spice mix:
2¹/₂ tablespoons salt
2¹/₂ tablespoons paprika
2 tablespoons garlic powder
1¹/₂ tablespoons onion powder
1 tablespoon cayenne pepper
1 tablespoon dried oregano
1 tablespoon dried thyme
2 teaspoons coarse black pepper
1¹/₂ teaspoons white pepper

Chili garlic mayo:
¹/₂ cup mayonnaise
1 teaspoon chili garlic paste
¹/₄ teaspoon Jamaican jerk seasoning
1 large clove garlic, pressed

To prepare Louisiana spice mix: Toss together all ingredients in a small bowl, and set aside.

To prepare chili garlic mayo: Whisk together all ingredients in a separate small bowl, and set aside.

To prepare chicken: Place Louisiana spice mix on a plate, and dredge both breasts in mix until fully coated. Melt butter in a heavy skillet. Place breasts in hot skillet, and cook over medium heat, about 4 minutes on each side. Set aside.

To make sandwiches: Split open and toast onion rolls. Spread with plenty of chili garlic mayo. Place chicken breasts on bottom half of each roll. Top each chicken breast with a piece of lettuce, tomato slice, 1¹/₂ tablespoons sour cream, jalapeño slices, and Tabasco sauce to taste.

Serves 2

Dan Aykroyd

Dan Aykroyd says he thinks like a blue collar worker—a mind-set he developed as a teen, working long, sweaty hours on a road crew in Canada's Northwest Territories. This work ethic haunts him and today Aykroyd crams his days with acting, writing, comedy, and the blues. A *Saturday Night Live* original, Aykroyd went on to star in *The Blues Brothers*, *Ghostbusters*, *Driving Miss Daisy*, and *North.* The Canadian native is also a successful businessman. In 1993, Aykroyd and partners opened a House of Blues club in Cambridge, Massachusetts, followed by clubs in New Orleans, Hollywood, and other locales. Aykroyd feels an almost supernatural influence from a fourteenth-century British ancestor, who was a police constable. Aykroyd is a police buff; he collects police badges, rides shotgun with detectives in squad cars, and owns a retired police motorcycle.

Ed Bangs

Ed Bangs worked his way through college as a furniture mover, feedlot hand, and oil field roughneck. At the end of that string of jobs was his dream—a career as a wildlife biologist. He cut his research teeth working in Alaska's Kenai National Wildlife Refuge, where he surveyed Dall sheep, mountain goats, loons, and salmon, and helped reintroduce caribou to the refuge. In 1991, Bangs was given what at the time seemed to be an impossible job—preparing westerners for wolf recovery. Bangs, the Gray Wolf Project leader, is credited with forging the compromises that made it possible to balance the biological needs of wolves with the economic realities of ranching families.

Granny's Apple Dumplings

This quintessential cold-weather dessert is well worth the effort. What a great way to end a winter feast or "wolf it down" for breakfast the following morning.

4 large Granny Smith apples
pastry for 4 (10-inch) pie crusts
2 cups brown sugar, divided
2 1/2 teaspoons cinnamon, divided
1/2 cup (1 stick) butter
3 cups sugar

Preheat oven to 375°. Butter a 9x13x2-inch baking pan, and set aside.

Using a small paring knife, core and peel the apples, then cut each one into 8 slices. Set aside.

Using a rolling pin, roll out the 4 pie crusts on a lightly floured surface into four 10x8-inch pieces. Place 8 apple slices side by side in the center of each pastry crust. Cover each batch of apple slices with 1/2 cup of brown sugar. Sprinkle each batch, including the crust, with 1/2 teaspoon of cinnamon. Place 2–3 pats of butter on each set of apple slices. Fold the long sides of each pastry over to cover the apples. Fold in the short ends and press to seal. Using a spatula, place each pastry in the pan, fold side up. The 4 dumplings should fit snugly next to each other. Dot the tops of each dumpling with butter, and sprinkle with cinnamon.

Bring 3 cups of water to a boil in a medium saucepan. Add the sugar, and stir to dissolve. Pour mixture over the dumplings until completely covered. (Too much syrup is better than too little.) Bake for 1 hour and 15 minutes. Let cool in the pan at least 1 hour. Serve in slices with a dollop of whipped cream or ice cream, if desired.

Serves 6–8

Ed Bangs

Dave's Toast
with Peanut Butter

**Dave
Barry**

This is a hearty snack that I generally enjoy 30 or 40 times per day when I'm supposed to be writing a column. —D.B.

You get yourself a slice of white bread, the kind with no fiber or vitamins or anything else healthy in it, and you put it in your toaster and push the lever down. I like my toast well done, so I push the lever down 3 or 4 times, until the smoke detector is beeping. Then I get a spoon and smear a fist-size gob of Peter Pan brand peanut butter (creamy, NOT chunky!) on the toast and eat it.

HINT: If you're in a hurry, you can skip the toast and put the peanut butter straight into your mouth.

ADDITIONAL HINT: If you're in a REAL hurry, you can also skip the spoon.

Serves 1

Dave Barry was born in 1947, and has been steadily growing older ever since, without actually reaching maturity. Barry went to Haverford College, where he was an English major and wrote lengthy scholarly papers filled with sentences that even he did not understand. Finally in 1983, Barry took a job with the *Miami Herald*, and he is still there, although he never answers the phone. In 1988, pending a recount, he won the Pulitzer Prize for commentary. His column appears in several hundred newspapers, yet another indication of the worsening drug crisis. Barry lives in Miami with his family and dogs: a large main dog, Earnest; and a small auxiliary dog, Zippy. Make him an offer.

Rick Bass

Rick Bass knows how to find oil. But the geologist-turned-author is not looking for it anymore. Now, Bass is seeking the right words. The Texas native wrote *Oil Notes*, *Winter: Notes from Montana*, and *The Lost Grizzlies: A Search for Survivors in the Wilderness*. In his book *The Ninemile Wolves*, Bass chronicled the appearance of a wolf pack in Montana's Ninemile Valley. The book is the result of years of study and hundreds of interviews and is laced with Bass' opinions about wolf reintroduction and recolonization. His inspired words lead the reader on an emotional journey into man's relationship with nature. Bass lives with his wife, artist Elizabeth Bass, and daughter Mary Katherine in the isolated Yaak Valley of northern Montana.

Yaak Valley Jalapeño Chicken and Dumplings

The chicken part of this recipe was given to us by friends and the dumpling part was added by my wife. It goes good with or without an awful lot of white wine. It's a good way to put a bit of fat back into your diet, and store up reserves in case you are planning, say, to expend a lot of energy writing letters to Congress telling them to protect the vast federal wildlands of the Yaak Valley, Montana.

Soup:
1 whole chicken (3–4 pounds), cut into pieces
2 or 3 jalapeño peppers, cored, seeded, and minced
2 cloves garlic, finely minced
2 green onions, chopped
2 thin slices of fresh ginger, 1 inch long
3 tablespoons chopped celery
1 tablespoon chopped cilantro

Dumplings:
1 1/2 cups all-purpose flour
2 teaspoons baking powder
3/4 teaspoon salt
pinch of sugar
3 tablespoons shortening
1/2 cup buttermilk
1/4 cup milk

Rinse chicken pieces well, and place in a large stock pot. Cover with cold water, then add all ingredients, saving the stamps for later. Bring to a boil over medium high heat, skim froth from the top, and lower heat. Simmer gently, uncovered, until chicken is tender and cooked through (about 1–1 1/2 hours).

Meanwhile, in a mixing bowl, sift together flour, baking powder, salt, and sugar. Using a pastry blender or your fingertips, cut in the shortening until the mixture resembles coarse crumbs. Stir in the milk and buttermilk until mixture is just moistened. Gather into a ball, and roll out 1/2 inch thick. Cut into 1-inch squares; dust squares with flour.

When chicken is done, strain and reserve stock, and remove ginger slices. Remove chicken pieces, let them cool, and take the meat off the bones, discarding the skin. Chop meat into small chunks and return to stock. Bring to a low boil, and add dumplings, one at a time. Cover, and simmer until dumplings are puffed and cooked through, about 15 minutes. Ladle into bowls, and serve immediately.

Serves 4

Monkey Bar Wild Rice Salad

This is one of Ed's favorite recipes from the popular Monkey Bar restaurant in Los Angeles, and is provided by executive chef Gordon Naccarato.

3 cups cooked wild rice or wild rice/basmati blend, chilled
1 pound assorted lettuces, cleaned and dried
1 bunch fresh cilantro, chopped, reserving 18 sprigs for garnish
1 teaspoon dried thyme
chopped fresh parsley to taste
salt and pepper to taste
1 roasted red bell pepper, julienned
1 avocado, peeled and sliced
3 tablespoons roasted slivered almonds
1 lemon, cut into wedges

Vinaigrette:
2 tablespoons champagne vinegar
2 tablespoons lemon juice
2 tablespoons minced shallots
1 teaspoon minced garlic
salt and pepper to taste
1/4 cup olive oil
2 tablespoons sesame oil

To prepare vinaigrette: Whisk together vinegar, lemon juice, shallots, garlic, and salt and pepper in a small bowl. Slowly drizzle in the oils, whisking constantly until smooth. Set aside.

To prepare salad: Arrange lettuces and cilantro on 6 plates. Place cooked rice in a medium bowl. Add herbs, and salt and pepper. Toss gently with vinaigrette to moisten. Spoon rice onto lettuce pieces and garnish with red peppers, avocado, and almonds. Place 3 sprigs of cilantro on each salad. Squeeze a fresh lemon wedge over rice and greens. Serve immediately.

Serves 6

Ed Begley Jr.

Dedicated environmentalist and Emmy nominee Ed Begley Jr. walks the eco-talk. At home, organic garbage is composted for the garden. If he can't ride his bike or take public transportation, the former *St. Elsewhere* physician drives his battery-powered Volkswagen Rabbit. He prefers trains for long-distance travel—they use less energy than planes. Begley's film credits include *She-Devil*, *The Accidental Tourist*, and *Even Cowgirls Get the Blues*. Begley serves on the board of ten national and local environmental groups.

Texas Bix Bender

Texas Bix Bender says you have to leave somewhere to get a geographical nickname. The author of *Don't Squat With Your Spurs On—A Cowboy's Guide to Life* does not live in Texas. If he did, no one would call him Texas. Bender is an ex-Marine, ex-bartender, ex-radio announcer, and ex-president of Mexico. (The latter is generally untrue, but worth a couple of drinks in almost any bar.) He resides in Nashville, Tennessee, is married to Saddlepal Sal, and drives a Buick pickup.

Texas Bix Bender

Madam Wazell's Roadhouse Steak

Madam Wazell is her name. Her father was Border Bill Wazell. He was a great admirer of the French language, but as you can plainly see from the name he gave his daughter, he never quite got a handle on it. This is her secret marinade. She used it to flavor up and tenderize the tasty steaks she grilled at her roadhouse in the Rio Grande Valley. She was a friend of the Hopi and the Navajo, and they called her She Wolf. I'm kinda careful around her myself. She's a good, honest, beautiful woman but not to be trifled with. When she gave me this recipe, she made me swear never to give it to anybody else—unless I made them swear to keep it a secret, too. So, before you read any further you have to swear never to give it to anybody else, unless you swear them to secrecy, too. This way we can keep it a secret. —T.B.B.

1¹/₂- to 2-pound flank steak or London broil

Marinade:
¹/₂ cup fresh cilantro, chopped as fine as your nerves will allow
juice from 1 lime
juice from 1 lemon
4 cloves garlic, crushed
2 tablespoons Worcestershire sauce
2 bay leaves
1 medium onion, finely chopped
2 tablespoons chili powder
1 tablespoon cayenne pepper
1 teaspoon ground cumin
¹/₄ cup olive oil
¹/₄ cup dry red wine (Madam Wazell prefers a Merlot)
¹/₄ cup red wine vinegar

In a large bowl, combine all of the marinade ingredients and whisk together. Trim any fat from the meat, and place in a shallow glass bowl or other nonreactive pan. Pour the marinade over the steak, coating evenly. Cover, and refrigerate overnight.

Prepare the barbecue for grilling. Grill the steak for about 6–7 minutes per side for medium-rare, depending upon the thickness of the meat.

Slice the meat at an angle, against the grain, into thin slabs.

Serves 4

Rice and Red Bell Pepper Soup

An ideal lunch on a snowy afternoon is a steaming bowl of this flavorful soup.

6 tablespoons olive oil
3 cups finely chopped onions
4–8 cloves garlic, finely chopped
4 red bell peppers, diced
8 cups vegetable or chicken stock
$^{1}/_{2}$ cup dry white wine
$^{3}/_{4}$ cup white rice
salt and pepper to taste
$^{1}/_{4}$ cup finely chopped fresh parsley for garnish

Heat olive oil in a soup pot. Add onions, garlic, and red peppers. Sauté, stirring frequently, over medium heat until wilted and soft, about 20 minutes.

Stir in vegetable or chicken stock, wine, and rice. Raise heat and bring to a boil. Cover and let simmer for about 30 minutes. Add seasoning, sprinkle with parsley, and serve.

Serves 6–8

Candice Bergen

Daughter of famous ventriloquist Edgar Bergen, Candice Bergen was born into a charmed world: holidays with "Uncle Walt" Disney, and adolescence in Swiss boarding schools. But, the Emmy-winning star of the CBS hit series *Murphy Brown* has never taken her birthright for granted; she has always felt the need to give something back. During the sixties, Bergen plunged into social causes. She slept-in at Alcatraz to protest the plight of Native Americans, campaigned for antiwar candidates, and became a board member of Friends of the Earth. The unpretentious Bergen continues to give, working with environmental organizations and the Starlight Foundation, which grants wishes to dying children.

Rick LaBranche 1993

Chris Berman

In 1979, one month after its inception, ESPN hired a little-known, twenty-four-year-old sports anchor named Chris Berman. Since then, Berman has established himself as one of television's most popular sportscasters. He has been selected National Sportscaster of the Year three times by his peers. He hosts *NFL PrimeTime*, Sunday night NFL telecasts, *Baseball Tonight*, and occasionally *SportsCenter*. Berman is famous for coining nicknames, including Roberto "Remember the Alomar," Bert "Be Home" Blyleven, Jim "Two Silhouettes On" Deshaies, and Von "Purple" Hayes. Berman's commentary of bronc riding is just as clever, although it's not heard on national television. He is one of the most entertaining fans in the stands at the Days of the Old West Rodeo in Hailey, Idaho, an event he attends every Fourth of July.

Baby Pork Back, Back, Back Ribs

I visit Idaho to white-water raft the Salmon River with my brother and his family. My brother's wife Kate is a fantastic cook and makes this, my favorite dish, when I'm in town. —C.B.

6 pounds baby back pork ribs
2 cups water

Sauce:
4 cups tomato ketchup (32-ounce bottle)
1/3 cup finely chopped onion
1/4 cup brown sugar
3 tablespoons lemon juice
3 tablespoons rum
3 tablespoons Worcestershire sauce
2 tablespoons Liquid Smoke™
2 teaspoons Tabasco sauce

Preheat oven to 350°.

Cut rib slabs in half, leaving 6–8 ribs per piece. In a large roasting pan, arrange ribs evenly, then add 2 cups of water. Cover pan very tightly with foil or lid to prevent steam from escaping. Bake for 3 hours, then drain and discard liquid.

Two hours into the baking time, combine all the sauce ingredients in a large saucepan. Simmer over low heat for 1 hour. Prepare grill.

Cover ribs with sauce, reserving about 1 1/2 cups for serving. Cook on barbecue approximately 5 minutes per side, or until slightly charred. Serve at once with reserved sauce on the side.

Serves 6

Chris Berman

Yellowstone Trout
with Pecans

This recipe came to me from my mother, Sue A. Bishop, who was born in Meridian, Mississippi, where pecans grow everywhere. —N.B.

2 fresh brook or rainbow trout (about 12 ounces each),
cleaned, heads and tails left on
$^{1}/_{2}$ cup pecan halves
2–3 tablespoons butter

Preheat oven to 400°.

Place trout in a large baking dish. Bake about 10–15 minutes. Skin should be crisp and fish opaque to the bone.

Five minutes before serving, sauté the pecans in butter in a small saucepan over low heat. Place the trout on warmed plates, and pour the pecan butter over the top.

Serves 2

Norm Bishop

Norm
Bishop

As a resource interpreter for Yellowstone National Park since 1980, Norm Bishop has educated thousands of visitors. Bishop first heard a wild wolf howl in 1988 in Prince Albert National Park, Saskatchewan, Canada. Four years later, while camping in the Boundary Waters Canoe Area, he heard a faint, distant howl. He believes he would have forgotten the howl if he hadn't noted it in his journal. Next time he hears a wolf howl in Yellowstone, Bishop says, he won't have to write it down to remember it. The tall, wiry Nordic racer says that when wolves are established in the nation's oldest and most popular park, his job will be done and he will retire.

Bonnie Blair

Bonnie Blair is the alpha-female of the sports world. The youngest of six children, Blair first stood on skates when she was two years old. Capturing five gold medals, she has won more gold than any American woman in the Olympics, summer or winter.

Blair's secret: Up at dawn, eat, stretch, sprint, eat, nap, stretch, workout without skates, eat, crash. Her idea of a party: a family dinner with the Blair Pack or "Da Blairs" as they are known in their hometown of Champaign, Illinois.

The World's Best Cookies

These crisp, nutty cookies are delicious, and just right for dunking in coffee. Bonnie recommends mixing everything with your hands …"it's easier."

1 cup (2 sticks) butter or margarine, softened
1 cup sugar
1 cup light brown sugar
1 egg
1 teaspoon vanilla extract
1 cup salad oil
3 1/2 cups all-purpose flour
1 cup Kellogg's Corn Flakes
1 cup rolled oats
1 cup shredded coconut
1/2 cup chopped pecans
1 teaspoon baking soda
1 teaspoon salt

Preheat oven to 325°.

In a large mixing bowl, cream together butter and sugars until fluffy. Add the egg, vanilla, and oil. Mix well. Add all remaining ingredients, and combine well.

Drop by rounded spoonfuls, about 1 inch apart, onto ungreased cookie sheet. Bake for 12–13 minutes. Cool on a wire rack.

Makes 36 cookies

Zucchini Spaghetti de Roma

*I have watched wolves feeding at night on the garbage dumps
around Rome. Guess what they were eating? Spaghetti, of course.
Aren't they Italian after all? —L.B.*

¹/₃ cup olive oil
1 pound fresh zucchini, washed and thinly sliced
1 teaspoon salt
¹/₄ cup chopped fresh parsley
¹/₂ teaspoon dried saffron
¹/₂ cup warm milk
1 pound spaghetti or linguine
fresh grated Parmesan cheese to taste

Bring a large pot of water to a boil.

Heat the olive oil in a medium skillet. Add the zucchini, and sauté over medium heat, making sure it doesn't burn. Add a teaspoon of salt and the parsley. Cook zucchini until golden, 10–15 minutes.

When the zucchini slices are almost cooked, stir the saffron into the warm milk. Add the pasta to the boiling water. Just a reminder on how to cook spaghetti Italian style: Always use lots of boiling water, and stir for the first minute to make sure the spaghetti is all under water. Now monitor the cooking: Test the spaghetti after about 8 minutes, and continue to test it every minute after that until it is "al dente," which means that the inner part of the spaghetti is still a bit hard to the bite.

When the spaghetti is cooked "al dente," drain it in a colander, and put it into a large, warmed serving dish. Pour the zucchini and the saffron/milk mixture over it, and mix well. Add Parmesan cheese to taste. If the spaghetti is too dry, add some olive oil. Serve immediately.

Serves 4

Luigi Boitani

When professor Luigi Boitani describes the state of Italian wolves to North American audiences, he is usually met with wonder and disbelief. Many people are amazed that there are wild wolves in his crowded country. Today an estimated 400 wolves live in the Apennine range and close to large cities like Rome and Florence. Wolves can live almost anywhere there is prey—deer, elk, bison, moose, or pasta. Working out of the University of Roma, Boitani is a leader in Italian wolf research.

Diane Boyd

If you're trying to reach Diane Boyd, don't bother with a cellular or princess phone, fax, or e-mail. This petite biologist lives without electricity in a log cabin in the mountains near Glacier National Park. Boyd's research on the Glacier wolf population distinguishes her among the nation's top wolf biologists. Her graduate degree studies of the first lone wolf in the park have evolved into a consuming passion. It began in 1979, when she tracked the loner, and later his mate and several generations of descendents through the Rockies.

Glacier Huckleberry Delight

Fresh huckleberries are in season during July and August and can often be found in the historic regions of the gray wolf. They have a distinctly sweet, winy taste, and are worth searching for. Use blueberries, raspberries, or any other fresh berry if you can't find the huckleberries.

6 cups fresh huckleberries, rinsed, drained, and picked over
1¹/₂ cups sugar
4 tablespoons cornstarch
1¹/₂ cups all-purpose flour
1¹/₂ cups rolled oats
1 cup brown sugar
¹/₂ cup butter, melted
1 teaspoon ground cinnamon
¹/₄ teaspoon grated nutmeg

Preheat oven to 350°.

In a large mixing bowl, combine huckleberries, sugar, and cornstarch. Spread this mixture evenly into a 9x13-inch baking pan.

Combine all other ingredients in a medium bowl, and sprinkle this topping over the berry mixture. Bake for 30 minutes, or until well browned and bubbly hot. Serve warm.

Serves 4–6

Ravenwood Pasta with Marinated Artichoke Hearts

Jim Brandenburg

*Using a spinach or tomato-based pasta gives this
well-rounded sauce a festive touch.*

6-ounce jar marinated artichoke hearts (I usually add more)
1 tablespoon olive oil
1 tablespoon butter
1 cup sliced yellow onions
1 tablespoon dried basil
$\frac{1}{2}$ cup sour cream
$\frac{1}{2}$ cup cottage cheese
8 ounces pasta (fettuccine, tagliatelle, or other wide pasta works well)
chopped fresh parsley or basil for garnish

Anthony Brandenburg

Drain the liquid from the marinated artichokes into a large skillet. Slice the drained hearts into bite-sized pieces and set aside.

Add the olive oil and butter to the marinade in the skillet. Heat this mixture. Add the onions, and sauté them over medium heat until soft, about 5–8 minutes. Add the artichoke hearts and basil, and sauté 3–5 minutes more. Remove from heat, stir in sour cream and cottage cheese, and cover.

Cook and drain the pasta, then toss immediately with the warm sauce. Sprinkle with fresh parsley or basil. Add salt, pepper, cayenne or chile peppers, and Parmesan cheese to your liking.

Serves 2–4

In 1991, the United Nations presented Minnesota photographer Jim Brandenburg with a World Achievement Award for using nature photography to raise public awareness of the environment. Two of Brandenburg's books, *Brother Wolf: A Forgotten Promise* and *White Wolf: Living with an Arctic Legend*, are considered to be definitive photographic works documenting wolf behavior. In *Brother Wolf*, he turned his camera on the timber wolves that haunt the forests near Ravenwood, his cabin in the far reaches of northern Minnesota's Boundary Waters Canoe Area.

Curried Egg Appetizer

Dorothy and Lloyd Bridges

Dorothy and Lloyd Bridges met more than sixty years ago, when both were UCLA students interested in acting. Dorothy Bridges is credited with keeping her family on an even keel while other Hollywood families drifted apart. Their sons, Jeff and Beau, appeared on Lloyd's long-running television series *Sea Hunt*. After years spent as the star of *Sea Hunt*, Lloyd is especially devoted to groups that protect the sea, such as American Oceans Campaign, Whales Alive, and EarthTrust, of which he is honorary president.

When our children were growing up, we tried to teach them kindness to animals. I often wrote poems for them. Here's one:

> *Never bother dogs*
> *While they eat their food*
> *Pulling cats by tails*
> *Shows that you are rude*
> *Squashing bugs for fun,*
> *(Ones that won't hurt you),*
> *Isn't very nice,*
> *Nor kind thing to do.*
> *Animals can feel,*
> *Just like you and I.*
> *Suppose some great big giant*
> *Went and made you cry?*

The following recipe is a good one to have in your file, because you usually have all the ingredients on hand when you must come up with an appetizer on short notice. —D.B.

1/4 cup cold water
1 tablespoon unflavored gelatin
1 chicken-flavored bouillon cube
boiling water
2 hard-boiled eggs
3/4 cup mayonnaise
1 teaspoon curry powder
1 tablespoon chopped fresh parsley
salt to taste
chopped onion to taste
watercress or parsley for garnish

Pour cold water in a 1-cup measuring cup. Stir in gelatin to dissolve. Add bouillon cube and boiling water to the 3/4-cup mark. Stir well, and refrigerate until cool.

In a medium bowl, mash together eggs, mayonnaise, curry, parsley, and salt and onion to taste. Add to cooled gelatin mixture. Stir together and pour into a 2-cup mold. Chill until firm. To unmold, dip the outside of the mold into a bowl of warm water, and turn out onto a serving dish. Garnish with watercress and serve with crackers.

Serves 6

Montana Granola

A hearty breakfast mix that will stay with you through a morning run on mountain trails. You can also stash it in your backpack for an afternoon snack, or enjoy it with steamed milk while curled up on the sofa in front of a warm fire.

1–2 cups pitted dates, prunes, raisins, or other fruit combination
4 cups old-fashioned oats
1 cup shredded coconut
1 cup walnuts or pine nuts
1 cup wheat germ
$^1/_3$ cup sesame seeds
$^1/_2$ cup honey
$^1/_2$ cup oil (canola or any vegetable oil)

Preheat oven to 325°.

Snip dried fruit into small pieces and set aside. In a large bowl, combine oats, coconut, nuts, wheat germ, and sesame seeds. Set aside.

Combine honey and oil in a medium saucepan. Bring mixture to a boil while stirring over medium heat. Pour the honey/oil combination into the oatmeal mixture, and blend well. Divide new mixture between two 9x13-inch baking pans. Bake for 25 minutes, stirring every 5–10 minutes to avoid burning. Toss in fruit when cool. Store in an airtight container for best results.

Makes approximately 1$^1/_2$ pounds granola

Tom Brokaw

In addition to being a respected newsman and enduring NBC anchor, Tom Brokaw is a climber, wild world adventurer, and runner. His favorite place on the globe to run is a dirt road in sight of the Bear Tooth Mountains near his Montana home. Brokaw joined NBC News in 1966, and has received numerous awards for his reporting, including an Emmy. While the South Dakota native supports protecting threatened and endangered species like the grizzly bear and the gray wolf, he also understands the pressures traditional American ranch families feel in the new West.

Jackson Browne

Frank Ockenfels 3

Born in Heidelberg, West Germany, Jackson Browne was raised in Los Angeles, where he studied piano and guitar as a boy. By his late teens he was a driving member of the Nitty Gritty Dirt Band. With his emotionally poetic verse, Jackson has confronted what's important in his life through his music. In the late 1970s, he cofounded MUSE, Musicians United for Safe Energy, which opposed the proliferation of nuclear power, and set an early precedent for the music industry's growing political consciousness. In 1986, *Lives in the Balance* sounded the alarm about U.S. policy in Nicaragua. *I'm Alive* reflects the human condition with grace and brilliance and *Looking East* returns to politics.

Norwegian Pancakes

My grandmother came to Minneapolis from Norway when she was a young girl and for many years was the house mother of a fraternity at the University of Minnesota. Her recipe for Norwegian pancakes comes from a book of handwritten recipes my mother gave to me and my son, Ethan. These can be served various ways: with powdered sugar and jelly, with syrup and a soft fried egg on top, or with fruit and yogurt. My favorite is with a little bit of powdered sugar and lemon. —J.B.

3 eggs
1¹/₂ cups milk
1 cup flour
¹/₂ teaspoon salt
1 tablespoon oil or butter, melted

Place eggs in a medium mixing bowl, and beat well. Add milk, flour, and salt. Combine until smooth.

Preheat a large griddle over medium heat. Add the oil, and pour in enough batter to make 3 or 4 pancakes about 4 inches in diameter. When both sides are slightly browned, stack on a warmed plate. Keep them in a warm oven until you have made enough for each person.

Makes approximately 20 pancakes

Margaritaville
Key Lime Pie

A classic. This tangy dessert will summon images of warm tropical days and sunshine drenched beaches. Sail away!

4 eggs, separated
¹/₂ cup bottled Key lime juice
14-ounce can sweetened condensed milk
9-inch graham cracker pie shell, baked according to directions
¹/₂ teaspoon cream of tartar
¹/₃ cup sugar

Preheat oven to 350°.

In a medium mixing bowl, beat egg yolks until light and thick. Blend in lime juice and milk. Transfer to a medium saucepan, and cook over low heat until mixture thickens, about 5–7 minutes. If desired, add a few drops of green food coloring. Pour mixture into pie shell.

Using an electric mixer, beat egg whites and cream of tartar until stiff, about 3 minutes. Gradually beat in sugar until glossy peaks form. Spread this mixture over surface of pie to edge of crust. Bake until golden brown, about 20 minutes. Chill at least 2 hours before serving.

Serves 8

HOWLIN WITH THE WOLVES

Jimmy Buffett

Ray Stanyard

Jimmy Buffett

From his grandfather, a sea captain, Jimmy Buffett learned that all creatures have their place within nature's delicate balance. Ten years ago, he started a movement to save the manatee—a pudgy, docile, and curious sea mammal. Today, the 30,000-member Save the Manatee Club is a leader in the race to protect the endangered species. Buffett's musical roots lie in New Orleans, and he hasn't missed a Jazz Fest there in twenty years. After decades of success in the music business, Buffett wrote the best-selling *Where is Joe Merchant?*, a Caribbean adventure and love story about a seaplane pilot.

Tantoo Cardinal

Long a celebrity in her native Canada, Tantoo Cardinal didn't gain national recognition in the United States until she played Blackshawl, the medicine man's wife in *Dances with Wolves*. *Legends of the Fall* and *Where the Rivers Flow North* followed. Proud of her Cree and European blood, Cardinal says, "When we talk about the wolf, the West, and the environment, it reminds me of a generational upheaval we of native spirit are born into. We search for the environment that is home. We inherit the struggle of our ancestors—reminding ourselves of our responsibility to take care of that which is loaned to us for the next generation."

Rhubarb Bread

Delicious and suitably tart, this bread is simple to make. It's sweetened with honey and orange juice instead of sugar, and makes a moist and healthy loaf. Frozen rhubarb may be substituted if fresh is not available.

1 egg
1 cup honey
1/2 cup butter, melted
1/2 cup orange juice
1 1/2 cups finely chopped fresh rhubarb
3/4 cup chopped walnuts or pecans
2 1/2 cups all-purpose flour
2 teaspoons baking powder
1/2 teaspoon baking soda
1/2 teaspoon salt
1/4 teaspoon powdered ginger
1/4 teaspoon ground cinnamon

Preheat oven to 350°. Butter 2 small loaf pans.

In a large mixing bowl, beat together the egg, honey, melted butter, and orange juice. Stir in the rhubarb and nuts.

In a separate large bowl, sift together the flour, baking powder, baking soda, salt, ginger, and cinnamon.

Combine dry and wet ingredients, stirring just to mix. Pour the batter into prepared pans, and bake for 35–40 minutes, or until the tops feel springy to the touch. Cool bread in pans for 10 minutes before removing to cool on a rack.

Makes 2 small loaves

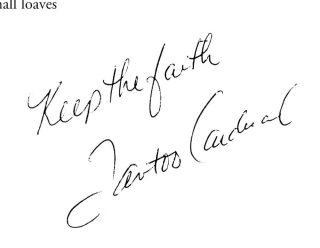

Mexican Polenta Pie

An earthy dish that can be served on the side or as a vegetarian entrée. If you are a meat eater, shredded grilled chicken or beef makes a wonderful addition.

2 tablespoons safflower oil
1 small onion, coarsely chopped
8 ounces mushrooms, thinly sliced
1 teaspoon cumin seeds
1 teaspoon chili powder
1/4 teaspoon crushed red pepper
28-ounce can plum tomatoes, drained (or use fresh, seeded)
16-ounce can black beans, rinsed and drained
4-ounce can chopped mild green chiles, drained
3/4 teaspoon salt
2/3 cup instant polenta
1/2 cup grated sharp Cheddar cheese

Preheat oven to 400°.

Heat oil in a large skillet over medium-high heat. Add the onion and cook, stirring occasionally, until slightly softened, about 3 minutes. Stir in the mushrooms, cumin seeds, chili powder, and crushed red pepper. Cook, stirring periodically, until the mushrooms soften and release juices, about 3 minutes.

Crush the tomatoes, and add them to the skillet. Add the black beans and green chiles. Reduce heat to medium, and simmer for 10 minutes. Stir in 1/4 teaspoon of the salt. Drain this mixture a little if overly runny.

Meanwhile, in a 10-inch ovenproof skillet, combine 2 cups water and the remaining 1/2 teaspoon salt. Bring to a boil over high heat, and stir in the polenta. Reduce heat to medium-low and cook, stirring constantly, until the polenta holds its shape, about 6 minutes. Remove from heat, and set aside for 5 minutes.

Spread the black bean chili mixture evenly over the polenta. Sprinkle the cheese on top. Bake for 15 minutes, until the chili is bubbling and the cheese is melted. Let cool for 15 minutes before serving. Cut into 4 even slices, and use a spatula to remove from skillet.

Serves 4

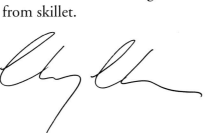

Chevy Chase

"I'm Chevy Chase and you're not ..." That smart-aleck remark along with his deadpan delivery and slapstick antics propelled Cornelius Crane "Chevy" Chase to fame as the anchor of *Saturday Night Live's Weekend Update*. Chase has been known to be serious, but only occasionally. One of his more academic pursuits is an advisory position, officially titled the Environmental Guru, to the Center for Environmental Education. His wife, Jayni, founded the organization in 1989. The nonprofit Center houses one of the nation's most comprehensive environmental lending libraries, containing over 7,500 periodicals, books, and videos.

the pack

wolves live in societies of three to fifteen extended family members. Leading the family is the alpha, or dominant, pair. The alpha male and alpha female are usually the most aggressive and direct the activities of the entire pack. Subordinate wolves—aunts, uncles, cousins, and pups—make up the rest of the family. Typically, the only wolves to mate within the pack are the alphas. This hierarchy keeps the size of the pack in check, assuring that the number of wolves in a given area does not exceed the prey base, or food availability.

The alphas begin courting in winter, and by early spring, four to six pups are born. The entire pack pitches in to raise the pups. The nonbreeding, lower-ranking wolves baby-sit and roughhouse with the pups, teaching them what they need to know. Pup discipline, handed out sparingly, is firm but not harsh. When an adult is fed up with an annoying pup, he might gently pin the youngster to the ground until it yelps.

Wolves are social animals, usually staying together all their lives. There appears to be a real sense of family among pack members. They are affectionate and friendly, nuzzling and licking each other. With tails wagging and smiles on their faces, they truly seem to enjoy kinship.

L. McNee Watson © '95

Jim Dutcher

pups

in the spring, a week or more before she whelps, the pregnant alpha wolf finds a den site. There, she gives birth to a litter, normally four to six pups. The pups, each weighing about a pound, are born blind, deaf, and helpless.

During the first four weeks, the mother wolf leaves the underground den only to drink water. The other wolves stay close to the den—guarding and watching the pups and bringing meat to the alpha female. Each wolf puts the pack ahead of himself during this time, sacrificing mobility and distant hunting for the sake of the pups and the nursing alpha female.

Wolf pups may begin howling before their eyes open at two weeks of age. The pups grow at an extraordinary rate, and by the time they are three weeks old, they are ready for a peek at life outside their womblike den.

Like energetic toddlers, the pups are curious and playful, with needle-sharp teeth for chewing on each others' tails and on an adult's scruff. The mother, or a baby-sitter, remains at the den to watch over the inquisitive pups when the other adults go off to hunt.

By late fall, the pups approach the height of an adult, although they do not weigh as much. A typical adult weighs between 80 and 110 pounds, but can weigh as much as 175 pounds. The pups are ready to accompany the mature wolves on nearby hunts. Catching mice or even a snowshoe hare comes naturally to the pups, which have been playing pounce games for weeks. However, they must be taught the pack ritual of bringing down large animals like deer, moose, elk, and caribou.

The entire pack's participation in the gentle and watchful care of pups is one of the hallmarks of wolf behavior.

Jim Dutcher

Jim Dutcher

hierarchy

wolves appear to be born with distinct personalities. Some are clowns, foolish and lazy. Others are born leaders with aggressive, take-charge attitudes—CEOs from the time they toddle out of the den. It is these personality types that make up the hierarchy of the pack. The leaders rise to alpha status, while others fulfill a lower rank.

Establishing and maintaining social order within the pack is a continual process. Wolves repeatedly challenge one another by displays of aggression. Anyone who has observed domestic dogs will recognize the body language of submission and dominance. The dominant, or alpha, wolf assertively stands over a subordinate. His ears are pitched forward and his tail held confidently high. A submissive animal slumps, his tail curled between his legs and his ears tucked back. There are many such obvious displays and many other subtle signals that are part of the wolf's dance for position.

Being an alpha has its advantages. The alpha male and alpha female are usually the only pair in a pack to copulate and sire offspring. The alpha couple is almost always the first to eat after a kill. Some biologists suggest that alpha animals may carry more weight in the pack's group decisions about where to den, and where and when to hunt.

I recall how one Alaska evening, the sun still bright at 11:30 P.M., we watched three wolves slip over the flanks of a hill in the Brooks Range like rafts dipping over riffles on a river. Sunlight shattered on a melt pond ahead of them. Spotting some pintail ducks there, the wolves quickly flattened out in the blueberries and heather. They squirmed slowly toward the water. At a distance of fifty feet they popped in the air like corks and charged the ducks. The pintails exploded skyward in a brilliant confusion of pounding wings, bounding wolves, and sheets of sunburst water. Breast feathers from their chests hung almost motionless in midair. They got away. The wolves cavorted in the pond, lapped some water, and were gone. It was all a game.

—Barry Lopez, *Of Wolves and Men*

Francis Ford Coppola

Bearded and burly, Francis Ford Coppola is as charming and talented as he is bold and controversial. However, his artistic talents have never been disputed. He's been awarded five Oscars for his gifted screenwriting and directing abilities. The man who brought us *The Godfather* and *Bram Stoker's Dracula* is married to Eleanor Neil Coppola. She produced the impressive documentary, *Heart of Darkness*, about the making of Francis' *Apocalypse Now*. They live on a 100-year-old, 2,000-acre vineyard in California's Napa Valley, where Niebaum-Coppola wine is produced.

Coppola Family Onion Focaccia

Focaccia is a peasant flat bread from the Liguria area of Italy. It can be prepared with tomatoes, garlic, olives, or even fruit for a sweet version. This fast-baking bread is a Coppola family favorite.

Dough:
1 envelope active dry yeast (1 tablespoon)
1¹/₂ cups lukewarm water
1 tablespoon olive oil
1 teaspoon salt
4 cups all-purpose flour

Topping for 1 focaccia:
¹/₂ cup olive oil
3 large onions, sliced thinly
1 teaspoon chopped fresh parsley
salt and pepper to taste

To prepare the dough: In a small bowl, dissolve the yeast in warm water. Add oil and salt. Stir to combine.

Place the flour into a large mixing bowl. When yeast mixture starts to foam, add it to the flour, and combine with your hands until the dough holds its shape. Transfer the dough to a floured surface, and knead until it becomes smooth and elastic, about 5–10 minutes. Add a little more flour if dough becomes too sticky to handle. Form the dough into 3 balls. Using your hands, cover the top and bottom with olive oil. Place each ball in a separate small bowl. Cover with a damp cloth, and let rise in a warm location until doubled, about 1 hour.

When dough has risen properly, place in the refrigerator until ready to use. This dough will make three 8-inch pizzas or focaccias.

Preheat oven to 400°.

To prepare focaccia: Heat olive oil in a large skillet, and add onions. Sauté until caramelized and golden brown. Set aside.

Place 1 ball of dough on a lightly floured surface. Using a rolling pin, roll out dough to the size of a dinner plate. Transfer to an oiled baking sheet. Spread the onions evenly over the dough, sprinkle with the parsley, and salt and pepper to taste.

Take one end of the dough and fold it over to the middle. Take the other end, and do the same. Bake until crust is golden brown, about 20–25 minutes. Cut focaccia into 2¹/₂-inch slices, and serve hot.

Serves 4–6

Wild Dog
Spicy Lamb Stew

Eat lamb. 10,000 coyotes can't be wrong! —*P.C.*

1 cup dried white beans, rinsed and picked over
4 ounces smoked or slab bacon
4 large dried New Mexico chiles
2 dried chipotle chiles
3–4 tablespoons olive oil
1½ pounds boneless lamb shoulder, cut into 1½-inch cubes
salt and pepper to taste
1 medium onion, finely chopped
3–4 cloves garlic, finely minced
1½ tablespoons ground cumin
2 teaspoons each: chopped fresh thyme and oregano
28-ounce can crushed tomatoes
6-ounce can tomato paste
2 tablespoons sugar
1 bay leaf

Bring beans, bacon, and 4 cups water to a rolling boil in a medium saucepan. Remove from heat and let stand for 1 hour.

Place all the chile peppers in a large bowl. Cover with 3 cups hot water, and let soak for about 20 minutes. Drain the chiles, saving 1 cup of the water. Remove and discard the stems and seeds. Puree the chiles with the reserved water in a food processor. Strain this mixture through a sieve or colander back into the bowl, and set aside.

Heat the olive oil in a large soup pot. Brown the lamb in small batches, sprinkling with salt and pepper, about 5 minutes each batch. Remove meat from the pot, and set aside. Add the onion and garlic to the pot, and cook over medium-low heat until transparent, about 4–5 minutes. Stir in the cumin, thyme, and oregano. Cook for 2–3 minutes. Add the lamb, pureed chiles, crushed tomatoes, and tomato paste, and combine. Add sugar, bay leaf, and ¾ cup water, and bring to a boil over medium-high heat. Reduce heat, cover, and simmer for 1½ hours, stirring often. Remove and discard the bay leaf. After the stew has been simmering for 30 minutes, drain the white beans and bacon. Return them to their pan, add 6 cups of water, and bring to a boil. Lower heat, and simmer for 1 hour, or until tender. Drain. Chop the bacon into small pieces, and add to the stew, along with the beans. Combine well, and add salt to taste. Ladle over white rice.

Serves 6

Peter Coyote

Greg Gorman

In the 1960s, Peter Coyote scrounged for free food and distributed it to San Francisco's hungry as a member of the radically creative Haight-Ashbury group, The Diggers. In the mid-seventies, then-Governor Jerry Brown appointed him head of the California Arts Council. He has built a career as a movie and television actor, starring in such films as *E.T.*, *Jagged Edge*, *Outrageous Fortune*, and *Breach of Conduct*. Coyote's television credits include the environmentally informative *Return of the Wolves*, *The Grizzlies*, and *The New Range Wars*.

Jamie Lee Curtis

In her hurried scrawl, Jamie Lee Curtis describes herself: "JLC is a mother, daughter, sister, wife, writer, director, driver (stick and manual), snowboarder, inventor, and **WOLF LOVER.**" She doesn't mention *A Fish Called Wanda*, *True Lies,* or the other film roles that have brought her critical acclaim. At home at the base of the Boulder Mountains, Curtis drives an old Toyota Landcruiser and retreats from the limelight, except for an occasional public appearance for Idaho's wildlife.

Happy Marriage Stew

1 black dress (short if in season)
1 pair black heels
1 dab cologne
1 phone (touchtone is quicker)
1 sleepover date for child (away from home)
1 "Names and Numbers" phonebook
1 candle
1 bottle of wine (optional)
1 music source
1 major credit card, or cash if you can find it
Piccolo roasted chicken to go*

Combine all of the above. Preheat electric blanket to high. Turn music to low. Turn phone off. Perfume to taste, and *Voilà!* —J.L.C.

**Piccolo Roasted Chicken

This wonderful recipe was given to us by Abby Grosvenor, the proprietor of Piccolo, an Italian country restaurant in Ketchum, Idaho.

2 cups good-quality olive oil
3 or 4 fresh rosemary sprigs
5 whole cloves garlic, peeled
2 chickens (2½–3 pounds each), rinsed, patted dry, and cut in half
salt and pepper to taste
½ cup dried rosemary

Combine olive oil, fresh rosemary sprigs, and garlic cloves in a jar, and allow to steep overnight. Next day….

Preheat oven to 475°.

Line a sheet pan with foil, and place the chickens, skin side up, on the pan. Brush halves very generously with the garlic-rosemary oil, and sprinkle with salt and pepper. Scatter the dried rosemary over the chickens. (The halves will look furry.) Drizzle with a little more olive oil, and bake 45–50 minutes, or until sizzling and dark golden brown.

Serves 4

Wild Idaho Potato Kugel

This crispy kugel is reminiscent of potato latkes, which are traditional throughout northern and eastern Europe. The variation here is that it's baked instead of fried. These are great when plain mashed potatoes just won't do.

4–5 medium potatoes, peeled
2 eggs, lightly beaten
1/2 cup all-purpose flour
1/2 cup butter or margarine, melted
1 tablespoon finely chopped onion
1 heaping teaspoon baking powder
1 heaping teaspoon salt
1/2 teaspoon ground caraway seeds
1/2 teaspoon dill weed
freshly ground black pepper to taste

Preheat oven to 400°. Grease a 13x9x2-inch casserole.

Grate potatoes into a large mixing bowl. Let them sit for 15 minutes. The potatoes will release liquid and turn red. Transfer them to a colander and rinse thoroughly with water. Squeeze them to remove as much water as possible, and transfer them back to the clean mixing bowl.

Add all other ingredients, and combine well. Spread evenly in the casserole, and bake for 45 minutes, or until golden brown. Cut into individual slices, and serve immediately.

Serves 4–6

Dan Davis

Dan Davis

When a lone male wolf wandered from Glacier National Park into the Selway-Bitterroot Wilderness in 1990, biologists darted and put a radio collar on him. From that time until the battery died almost four years later, the animal, named the Kelly Creek Wolf, was Dan Davis' baby. Wolves typically stick to open areas—along waterways, valleys, and gentle hills. But the Kelly Creek Wolf preferred the craggy, granite mountains and heavy forests of Clearwater County, making tracking by foot impossible. Davis followed the radio messages over the rough terrain from an airplane. Davis, a wildlife biologist for the U.S. Forest Service, proved that lone wolves were entering the state and staying. Davis lives with his own pack in Orofino, Idaho.

Doris Day

Since founding the Doris Day Animal League in 1977, Doris Day has been a tireless worker on behalf of the humane and loving care of animals. The girl-next-door, leading lady of the sixties continues to receive frequent offers for television and film projects. Day declines, preferring a self-imposed retirement that enables her to remain focused on animal advocacy. She lives in Carmel, California, with an ever-changing assortment of dogs she rescues, tends to, and then places in homes.

Sicilian Cheese Pasta Bake

Here is a wholesome, nonmeat dish that I really love. —D.D.

1 cup tiny pasta shells (or 2 cups medium-sized pasta shells)
3 tablespoons olive oil
1 medium eggplant, peeled and cut into 1/2-inch cubes
1 small onion, finely chopped
minced fresh garlic to taste
1/3 cup tomato sauce
1/2 cup halved black olives
1/4 cup chopped fresh parsley
2 teaspoons lemon juice
1/2 teaspoon dried basil
1/2 teaspoon dried marjoram
salt and pepper to taste
1/2 pound Monterey Jack cheese, grated
1 1/2 cups freshly grated Parmesan cheese

Preheat oven to 375°.

Cook pasta shells according to directions, and drain. Heat olive oil in a large skillet. Add the eggplant, onions, and garlic. Sauté over medium heat for about 8 minutes, stirring often.

Combine eggplant mixture with all the remaining ingredients, except for the Parmesan cheese. Turn this mixture into a 2-quart baking dish, and sprinkle with the Parmesan cheese. Bake, uncovered, for 30 minutes, or until golden brown and bubbling.

Serves 6

Great Chefs of Europe Sauce

This recipe was born out of frustration in getting my two sons to partake in the epicurean delight of well-prepared fish. They love garlic and mustard, so I went off to the laboratory. But I created a monster… now they insist on this sauce with every seafood meal. It's excellent on salmon and trout, and is always a hit with garlic lovers. What's in a name? A simple reminder that we all need sizzle as much as we need steak. —H.F.

¼ cup olive oil
¼ cup butter, melted
1 cup Dijon mustard
3 cloves garlic, finely chopped
1 cup minced fresh parsley
1 lemon (or 2 tablespoons juice)

In a medium bowl, combine olive oil and melted butter. Add mustard and mix well. Stir in garlic and parsley. Squeeze in juice from the lemon, and combine.

Taste is enhanced by chilling for 30 minutes. Sauce can be used as a marinade, or on fish while it is cooking, or dollop a spoonful on the fish after it is cooked.

This recipe yields sauce for 4 pounds of fish.
Serves 8

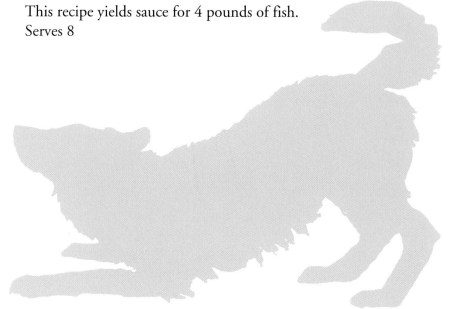

**Defenders
of Wildlife**

Defenders of Wildlife, under the guidance of Hank Fisher, has created the $100,000 Wolf Compensation Fund to reimburse ranchers in the Northern Rockies and the Southwest for all verified livestock losses to wolves. Defenders established the fund with private donations after wolves began crossing the Canadian border in the early 1980s and Montana ranchers experienced their first cattle and sheep losses in nearly fifty years. In the past, ranchers alone were forced to shoulder the cost of wolf depredation, causing animosity and ill will. By creating this fund, Defenders has been effective in diffusing the loudest and most ardent critics of wild wolves. Defenders' goal is to shift economic responsibility for wolf recovery away from the individual rancher and toward the millions of people who want to see the wolf in the wilds again.

Richard Dreyfuss

Richard Dreyfuss is a thinking person's actor, outspoken in his support of progressive causes and skilled in a vast range of roles from comedy to drama. He starred in three of the biggest movie hits of the seventies—*American Graffiti, Jaws,* and *Close Encounters of the Third Kind.* Later, *Always, Nuts,* and *Mr. Holland's Opus* proved his versatility.

Dreyfuss is proud that he was a conscientious objector during the Vietnam War, spending two years in alternate service as a clerk at Los Angeles County Hospital. Dreyfuss has opted to raise his children in the small town of Ketchum, Idaho. The Oscar-winning actor performs on the stage of Ketchum's community theater in support of local causes.

Seared Ahi with Sun Valley Mustard Sauce

When in Idaho, Richard enjoys taking his family to Sushi on Second in Ketchum. He doesn't ask for special treatment, preferring to slide up to the bar just like any other local. Chef Paul Sommerset has provided us with the recipe for one of Richard's frequently ordered favorites.

6 ounces fresh ahi tuna, as thick as possible (ask fishmonger for sushi-grade tuna)
2 tablespoons Hichimi (Chinese 7 spice, or substitute equal parts cayenne, paprika, and lemon pepper)
2 tablespoons sesame oil

Sauce:
¼ cup sake (or dry white wine)
¼ cup (total) finely diced green onions, garlic, and shallots
1 tablespoon Sun Valley Spicy Sweet or Jalapeño Mustard (or any other hot-sweet mustard)
¼ cup coconut milk
1 tablespoon butter
salt and pepper to taste

To prepare the sauce: Heat the sake or white wine in a medium sauté pan over medium-high heat. Add the onions, garlic, and shallots, and sauté until the wine is reduced by half. Stir in the mustard, and remove from heat. Add the coconut milk, and return to medium heat until sauce is reduced and slightly thickened. Add the butter, and stir until it's melted, producing a smooth sheen.

To prepare the tuna: Roll the ahi in the Hichimi, coating all sides. Heat the sesame oil in a medium sauté pan over high heat. When pan is very hot, grill the ahi as a single piece for 30 seconds to 1 minute per side, grilling all sides. (It will be crusty on the outside and rare and moist inside.) Allow to cool.

Use a very sharp knife that has been dipped in water. Cut the fish against the grain into ¼-inch slices. Arrange fanlike on plates, and drizzle warm sauce over fish, or place slices on top of the sauce.

Serves 2–4 as an appetizer

Wolf Camp Caesar Salad Dressing

This terrific version of Caesar dressing is Jim's favorite and one that he prepares weekly for the film crew at Wolf Camp. It's a much-anticipated treat after a long day of filming.

1 tablespoon mayonnaise
1 tablespoon Dijon mustard
a few drops of Tabasco sauce
a few drops of Worcestershire sauce
2-ounce can anchovy fillets with oil, diced (or less to taste)
juice of 1/2 lemon or 1 1/2 tablespoons bottled lemon juice
2 tablespoons white wine vinegar
2–3 large cloves garlic, pressed
3/4 cup olive oil

Whisk together mayonnaise and mustard. Add a few drops each of the Tabasco and Worcestershire. Stir in the anchovies along with the lemon juice and vinegar. Press the garlic into the mixture, and mix well with a fork. Add the olive oil, and blend well.

Makes 1 cup (enough for 6 dinner salads)

Jim Dutcher

Diana Walker

Filmmaker Jim Dutcher's Emmy award-winning *Wolf: Return of a Legend* left its more than seventeen million viewers bonded to the Sawtooth Pack and eagerly awaiting a sequel. Produced by ABC, the film chronicles a two-year period of the captive gray wolf pack in Idaho's Sawtooth Mountains. Dutcher captures one of the most moving moments in the history of wildlife cinematography—the pack, looking forlorn and listless, clearly mourning the death of the subordinate omega wolf, Motaki, after she is slain by a mountain lion. Dutcher believes that the wolf's survival in the modern world is dependent upon man's understanding of its complex social behavior.

Clint Eastwood

Eddie Adams/Sygma

Clint Eastwood has been the biggest draw in movie theaters for more than 20 years, earning a rumored $2 billion along the way. But for all his fame and fortune, he is still a no-bull-kinda guy. He drives a pickup, shuns the Hollywood elite, and dresses like the regular guys—a high-school teacher, an accountant, a salesman—who are his friends. His passions are film, jazz, golf, and skiing. Home is Carmel and Sun Valley. If you get up early on a stormy powder day at Idaho's famous ski resort, you might see Eastwood, an expert skier, disappear into the white stuff.

Spaghetti Western

Many of my cowboy movies were filmed in Italy, hence they became known as spaghetti westerns. A few years ago I participated in a gourmet gala, "The Flavors of Monterey" to benefit the March of Dimes. My truly edible "Spaghetti Western" brought me top honors! —C.E.

juice of 1 lemon
12 tablespoons (³/₄ cup) olive oil
12 baby artichokes
¹/₂ pound spaghetti
2 large cloves garlic, minced
¹/₄ cup finely chopped celery
4 tablespoons (¹/₄ cup) chopped shallots
¹/₂ cup tomato puree
¹/₂ cup fish stock
2 tablespoons chopped fresh parsley
2 tablespoons tomato paste
¹/₂ teaspoon anchovy paste
¹/₄ teaspoon thyme
1 bay leaf
1 teaspoon saffron threads
salt and freshly ground pepper
4 clams, chopped
4 prawns or jumbo shrimp
8 large sea scallops, quartered
12 large mussels
¹/₂ cup brandy
1 yellow bell pepper, thinly sliced
1 red bell pepper, thinly sliced
¹/₂ cup heavy cream
2¹/₂ tablespoons Pernod

Stir lemon juice and 2 tablespoons of olive oil into a large pot of boiling salted water. Add artichokes, and boil for 5 minutes, or until almost tender. Remove artichokes, and cool under cold running water. Reserve cooking water. Peel outer leaves from 8 artichokes down to the most tender part (set aside 4 artichokes with leaves intact). Cut off stems. Cut peeled artichokes into bite-sized pieces (about 1¹/₂ inches long). Set aside.

Add more salted water to leftover artichoke water, bring to a boil, and cook pasta according to directions. Drain pasta, and return to pot.

In a large skillet, heat 7 tablespoons olive oil. Sauté garlic, celery, and 2 tablespoons of the shallots over medium-low heat until golden. Stir in tomato puree, fish stock, parsley, tomato paste, anchovy paste, thyme, bay leaf, saffron, salt, pepper, and clams. Bring sauce to a simmer over low heat, and cover.

In large skillet, heat the remaining 3 tablespoons olive oil, and sauté the 2 remaining tablespoons shallots until golden. Season with black pepper. Add prawns, scallops, and mussels, then cover with brandy and ignite. Remove from heat. When flame subsides, stir this mixture into the sauce.

Add red and yellow peppers and the chopped artichokes, and simmer for 5 minutes. Pour in the cream and Pernod. Cook 1 minute, stirring constantly. Remove from heat.

Using a slotted spoon, remove peppers from sauce, and add them to the spaghetti. Rinse the spaghetti-pepper mixture in hot water and drain (this is to remove traces of the sauce).

Cover the bottom of 4 flat serving bowls with a few tablespoons of sauce. Arrange $1/4$ of the spaghetti in each bowl, leaving a well in the center. Place 2 quartered scallops in the center. Arrange 3 mussels on the edge of each plate, and on the opposite side, place 3 artichokes. Place a whole artichoke over the scallops. Spoon remaining sauce over the scallops and mussels, and place 1 prawn in the center. Serve immediately.

If preparing in advance, cover with foil, and set aside. To reheat, place in a preheated 325° oven for 20 minutes.

Serves 4

Environmental Media Association

Hopping Joyce

A traditional Creole New Year's dish made without the pork and sausage. It takes a while to prepare but does not need a lot of attention. It's typically served over white rice, but it's delicious with brown rice, too.

1¼ cups dried black beans, rinsed and picked over
4 cups water
½ teaspoon black pepper
¼ teaspoon crushed red pepper, or more to taste
5 cloves garlic, crushed
1 bay leaf
1¼ cups chopped onion

Place black beans and water in a stock pot, and bring to a boil. Boil for 2 minutes, remove from heat, and let stand 1 hour.

Add black pepper, red pepper, garlic, and bay leaf. Bring to a boil, uncovered. Reduce heat. Cover, and simmer for 1 hour, stirring occasionally.

Remove lid, and simmer, uncovered, until the beans are tender, and the mixture is thickened, about 40 minutes. Stir frequently.

Add onions, and continue to simmer for 20 minutes more. Remove bay leaf, and serve hot over warm rice.

Serves 6

Marushka Pinkola's Hungarian Goulash

Clarissa Pinkola Estés

Preamble to the recipe via long distance telephone between Clarissa and her 83- and 84-year-old foster parents, who are ethnic Hungarians:

Clarissa: Hello. I'm calling to get Mother's recipe for Hungarian Goulash. There's a very famous restaurant, Reiver's, near here that would like a recipe from the best Hungarian cook in America. That's you, Mama. Just tell me and I'll write it down for you.

Mama: I've been making this recipe for over 75 years. Of course I learned this by watching grandmama. That's the way you learn to cook. You stand there and watch. It's not easy. You have to stand there for a long time in the hot kitchen.

Dad: Ya, ya, you stand there and watch and have a few drinks. It's not easy. You have to drink a lot of wine for a long time in the hot kitchen.

Mama: Use 1 onion to a pound of meat.

Clarissa: How large is that onion, Mama?

Mama: You can't close your hand over it.

Clarissa: Is that about a ¹/₂ pound?

Mama: I don't know. I only know how big my hand is.
Sauté this onion in oil, but first chop up the onion coarsely.

Clarissa: How much oil, Mama?

Mama: Enough oil.

- Add meat (beef chuck) in ³/₄–1 inch cubes to onion, sauté until it turns from red to gray. Make the cubes bigger if you are serving people who labor outside. Make the cubes smaller if you are serving people who work in an office. If people are old or sick, shred the beef instead of cubing it.
- Smash or dice fine 2 little cloves of garlic, add to meat and onion.
- Add 1 tablespoon Hungarian Paprika (must be Hungarian Paprika or else it won't taste right).
- Add green pepper in ¹/₂ inch or less cubes; this can be hot or mild Cayenne, Hungarian or Jalapeño.

Clarissa: How much pepper, Mama?

Mama: If you want the people never to come back, put in a lot. If you like them a lot, put in as much as they like. If you have lovers, put in enough to make the man's eyes water and to make the woman sigh.

- Add 1 tablespoon flour to meat, onion, pepper, garlic, and paprika.
- Add 1–3 cups beef broth. If you want soup—you add more liquid (this is called *leves*). If you want stew, you add less liquid (then you have *gulas*—Americans call it goulash)
- Cook about an hour till meat is tender.
- Then add potatoes cubed to about 1 inch, and cook about 15 minutes and then test the potatoes to see if they are done. It depends on what kind of potatoes you use—some cook faster, some fall apart—try to get the ones that stay together so the *gulas* looks nice. You can also cook potatoes on the side, and then serve

Clarissa
Pinkola Estés

Clara Griffin

Since *Women Who Run With the Wolves* was published in 1992, Clarissa Pinkola Estés has been asked "eighty-blue-jillion times" if she lives with wolves. No, she quips, it was quite enough to have been raised by them. Estés, a distinguished poet, scholar, and psychoanalyst, says that the wolf is one of the most common animals that humans dream about. She believes society ignores this critical psychic fact in its current discussion about the wolf: When we eradicate living creatures from our environment, within a few generations they become *desaparecidos*; they are massacred in the dream world as well.

them with gravy over. Don't have them put my name on the menu, then if the goulash is not any good they won't know who gave them the recipe.

Clarissa: Mama, Carmone is an excellent cook. It's going to be very good.

Mama: Who is this Carmone?

Clarissa: He's the Chef at Reiver's. He's a very, very good cook.

Mama: Then he's Hungarian, yes?

Clarissa: In a previous life he was Hungarian. But in this life, he's Jamaican.

Mama: It's okay. If he's a good cook, he can be an honorary Hungarian.

Clarissa: I'll tell him. He'll be honored.

Mama: Just tell him not to cook the goulash until it's mush.

Clarissa: He knows how to do it right, Mama, I promise you.

Dad: Tell him I know his people; they have Red Stripe Beer.

Clarissa: I'll tell him, Dad.

Mama: Your dad says it's a good beer to drink for a long time in the hot kitchen.

Clarissa: No doubt. Thanks for the recipe, Mama. You know, I've got to go back to work now. I'll call you tomorrow, okay? I love you.

Mama: Okay, we love you, too.

Dad: We love you, too.

Mama: Tell that Carmone we love him, too.

Clarissa: I'll tell him, Mama.

Dad: Don't forget—tell him his people make good beer.

Clarissa: Okay, Mama and Dad. I'll tell him.

Mama and Dad: Don't forget.

Clarissa: I won't forget.

Mama and Dad: Don't forget.

Clarissa: Okay, I promise.

Dad and Mama: Okay, now we're going to hang up.

Clarissa: Okay, hang up now.

Dad and Mama: We're hanging up.

Clarissa: Okay, hang up now.

Dad and Mom: Okay, here we go. We're hanging up.

Clarissa: Okay, I love you, Goodbye.

Mama: Joszef, hang up the phone.

Dad: Marushka, I am hanging up the phone.

Click.

Click.

Click.

Serves 2–4

Buffalo in the Style of Tuscany

Buffalo is low in fat and high in protein. It is best cooked hot and fast; buffalo cooked to the well-done point is tough.

$1^1/2$ pounds buffalo tenderloin fillets (8 medallions, 1 inch thick)

Marinade:
$^1/2$ cup olive oil
2 cloves garlic, finely minced
1 tablespoon fresh rosemary leaves
1 tablespoon cracked black pepper
1 teaspoon fresh thyme leaves

Sauce:
2 tablespoons of the marinade, plus enough for sautéing
1 tablespoon anchovy paste, or 3 anchovy fillets
2 tablespoons capers
$^1/4$ cup pureed sun-dried tomatoes, or $^1/3$ cup tomato puree
$^1/4$ cup beef demiglace, or $^1/4$ cup beef stock
$^3/4$ cup Marsala wine
freshly ground black pepper

Place fillets in a shallow glass baking dish. Combine all marinade ingredients together in a small bowl, and pour over fillets. Let marinate at room temperature for 2–3 hours.

Pour enough marinade into a large skillet to thinly coat the bottom. Heat almost to the smoking point, and add the meat. Sear both sides until rare or medium-rare, about $2^1/2$–3 minutes for rare. Don't burn the oil, or it will impart a bitter flavor to the sauce. Remove medallions, and keep warm.

To the hot skillet, add the 2 remaining tablespoons marinade, anchovy paste, and capers. Stir, then cook briefly, and add the tomato puree. Reduce the mixture slightly. Add the demiglace and Marsala, and simmer until sufficiently thickened. Arrange medallions on plates, and spoon sauce on top. Add freshly ground black pepper to taste.

Serves 4

Jane Fonda and Ted Turner

1989 George Bennett

He is CNN, the America's Cup knight, the Goodwill Games, and a giant in global communication. She is the anti-war protester, the feminist, an Oscar winner, the aerobics guru, and finally a content fly-fishing wife. Together, they are one of the most powerful couples on the planet and they are both wolf advocates. Buffalo herds graze on their 300,000-acre Ladder Ranch near Truth or Consequences, New Mexico, and the 130,000-acre Flying D outside of Three Forks, Montana. They plan to turn the Flying D into a kind of privately owned national park. Fonda and Turner have now turned to the environment, population control, and peace as their ultimate challenge.

Peter Fonda

Peter Fonda spends most of his time on his Indian Hills Ranch in the Paradise Valley south of Livingston, Montana, where he farms alfalfa. Fonda and his wife, Becky, enjoy cooking, although she is the one who wins blue ribbons at county fairs. This laid-back Montana rancher role is a big change from Fonda's early role as a drug-fed adventurer in the generation-defining 1960s movie *Easy Rider*, for which he wrote the screenplay. The Fonda movie legacy continues with his daughter, Bridget Fonda. A Pisces, he is fond of sailing and the peacefulness of life along the Yellowstone River.

Indian Hills Ranch Lamb and Tomatoes

My favorite meals are often leftovers, or improvisations, as my wife, Becky, would call them. Be sure to serve a loaf of French or Italian bread to sop up the tomato and herb-flavored oil. —P.F.

2 cups cooked leg of lamb, cut into $^1/_2$-inch pieces
1–2 tablespoons finely minced garlic
salt to taste
$^1/_2$ teaspoon freshly ground pepper
4 tablespoons olive oil
$^1/_2$ cup fresh tomatoes, peeled, seeded, and cut into thin strips
$^1/_2$ cup thinly sliced scallions
$^1/_2$ cup coarsely chopped fresh parsley
1 teaspoon grated lemon zest
lemon quarters, for garnish

Combine lamb, garlic, salt, and pepper in a medium bowl. Mix together thoroughly. Choose a 10-inch heavy skillet that is attractive enough to bring to the table. Heat the olive oil in the skillet until it is very hot. Add the lamb mixture. Using a wooden spoon and stirring frequently, sear the cooked lamb over high heat, about 1–2 minutes. (Don't let it overcook or get tough.) Toss in the tomato strips and sauté for 2–3 minutes, or until just slightly cooked.

Using the spoon, push the meat and tomatoes to the center of the skillet. Surround them with the scallions and parsley in a ring. Sprinkle the meat with the lemon zest, and cover the pan tightly. Turn off the heat, and let the residual heat warm the herbs through.

After about 5 minutes, serve directly from the pan with a lemon wedge for each serving.

Serves 2

Curried Potato and Carrot Soup

A vegetarian, President Priscilla Feral believes that the healthiest, most compassionate, and ecologically responsible way to eat is to eliminate animal food products from our diets. This hearty and exotic soup is very simple to prepare.

4 tablespoons good-quality olive oil
1 medium yellow onion, thinly sliced
1 clove garlic, minced
6 cups vegetable broth or stock
5 medium potatoes, peeled and cut into 1-inch cubes
3 large carrots, peeled and diced
2 teaspoons curry powder
few dashes tamari or soy sauce
1/8 teaspoon powdered ginger
salt and pepper to taste

Heat olive oil in a large soup pot, and add onion and garlic. Sauté over medium heat until tender and lightly colored, about 10 minutes.

Add vegetable broth, potatoes, and carrots. Stir in all remaining ingredients and bring to a boil. Lower heat, and simmer for 20 minutes, or until potatoes are tender.

Remove soup from heat. Puree half the amount in a blender or food processor, and return the puree to the soup pot. Place the pot over low heat, adjust the seasonings, and heat through.

Serves 6

Friends of Animals

Friends of Animals led the 1992 Alaska tourism boycott—calling national attention to and stalling the state's wolf "control" program. Up to 75 percent of its wolf population was to be killed—baited, trapped, shot, and snared with the aid of snowmobiles, airplanes, and helicopters—in a 2,000-square-mile area south of Denali National Park. At howl-ins—public demonstrations for the wolf held in fifty-one cities around the country—tens of thousands of Alaska boycott postcards were distributed. The postcards, which said the sender would not travel to Alaska until the wolf control program was canceled, were later wheeled in by dollies to then-Governor Walter J. Hinkel's office. The state reinstated the program a year later, although national media coverage and subsequent public outrage quickly brought it to a temporary halt.

Steven Fritts

Steven Fritts is an Arkansas farm boy who somehow ended up studying wolves in the northern woods of Minnesota and later in Montana. Now, having spent more than two decades researching and managing wolves, Fritts, who has a doctorate in ecology, is considered the leading authority on wolves in the Northern Rockies. As the wolf recovery coordinator for the Northwest, Fritts laid the scientific groundwork for the release of wolves by the U.S. Fish and Wildlife Service in Yellowstone and Idaho.

Big Sky Pecan Tarts

This is one of our family's favorite desserts, and the one that always scores big when the biologists from our office get together for a little culinary socializing. —S.F.

½ cup plus 1 tablespoon butter, softened
3 ounces cream cheese, softened
1 cup all-purpose flour
¾ cup light brown sugar
1 egg
1 teaspoon vanilla extract
pinch of salt
⅔ cup chopped pecans
24 pecan halves for garnish

Preheat oven to 350°.

To prepare the pastry: Using a food processor, process the ½ cup butter, cream cheese, and flour until it forms a ball. Lightly dust a rolling pin with flour. On a floured board or countertop, roll out dough into a rectangle. Cut into 24 equal pieces, and shape into balls. Press into nonstick mini-tart pans, making 24 shells.

In a medium mixing bowl, combine the remaining tablespoon butter, brown sugar, egg, vanilla, and salt. Blend well. Stir in the chopped pecans, and place 1 teaspoon of filling into each shell. Top each with a pecan half. Bake for 25 minutes. Cool slightly, then carefully remove to a wire rack to finish cooling.

Makes 24 tarts

Wilderness Sweet Tooth Cookies

Pete's recipe was concocted after months living alone in a canvas tent in the wilderness, eating the same canned and freeze-dried foods for months without dinner conversation, or any conversation for that matter. This is a recipe for desperate times.

To Get Ready:

Read all the mountain man stories you can. Watch Robert Redford in *Jeremiah Johnson* again and again. In fanatical emulation, agree to spend the next seven months in a tent in the middle of some northern wilderness, in the winter, alone. It helps if you've never done this before. Also if you've never cooked before. Then, buy all your food for those seven months in one day. There'll be no refrigeration. Go heavy on cans and dry goods.

Get dropped off in the wilderness. Dig a hole to keep your food from freezing. Drop your food in the hole. Bury it. Eat rice and beans for the next few months.

Begin to realize how long it's been since you've eaten anything sweet. Anything at all. Try a spoonful of sugar, as in the song. Gag. Dig the Betty Crocker cookbook out from under your spare longjohns. Find you've only got all the ingredients for Brown Sugar Drops.

To Begin:

Stir up the ingredients. Brazenly add uncalled-for cinnamon. Stare for the first time at the tiny potbelly stove that is heating your tent. Wonder how to preheat it to 400. Look around, making sure no one can see you standing with a bowl of cookie batter, wishing for an oven. Remember you haven't seen anyone for months.

Get serious. From the woodpile, shovel out the old grill you found before the snow buried everything. Cut it to fit inside the stove. Use a file, because, before you came in, you couldn't see any reason to bring a hack saw. Scratch your head, trying to remember why you thought you'd need a file. Remember cookie batter instead.

Open stove and beat on wood, damping open flame. Decide it's 400 degrees. Spoon batter onto scrap tin sheet. Set on rack in stove. Close stove. Without timer, decide to go by smell. Step outside to enjoy another storm. Watch snow falling without wind, big flakes sifting down muffling the world. Tilt your head back and see from how high you can follow a single

Pete Fromm

During seven of the coldest months spanning 1977 and 1978, Pete Fromm, a college lifeguard and wanna-be mountain man, baby-sat two and a half million salmon eggs in the middle of Idaho's Selway-Bitterroot Wilderness. An Idaho wildlife agency hired Fromm to guard the eggs and to help ensure the survival of the rare salmon. The closest plowed road was 40 miles away; the closest person, 60. Fromm details the brutal cold, inhuman isolation, and fearful risks in the captivating story, *Indian Creek Chronicles: A Winter in the Bitterroot Wilderness*. The wildlife-biologist-turned-author lives with his family in Great Falls, Montana, and is a contributing editor of *Gray's Sporting Journal*. His other books include *The Tall Uncut* and *King of the Mountain: Sporting Stories*.

flake's descent. Again, check that no one is looking. Stick out your tongue and try catching only that flake. Laugh. Remember cookies. Jump into tent. Swear. Leave front flap of tent open to let out smoke.

Fill tin with new drops of cookie dough. Wait for fire to die out completely. Start second batch. Stay inside this time. Sit. Wait. Walk to open flap and shiver. Look at stump to see how much snow has accumulated.

Turn, with determination, back to stove. Sit in front of it. Flip through cookbook, wondering what you might try next. Guess you'll skip Coquilles St. Jacques.

At the very first hint of second batch of smoke, flip open stove and pull tin sheet out. Scrape blackened cookies onto table. Study them until cool enough to touch. Cut blackened bottoms off with a Buck knife. Repeat process on tops. Sides. Think, in road miles, how far it is to the dentist. Convert this to months. Eat brittle center morsel carefully, letting saliva soften the crunch. Decide not to do this twice.

Drop last of cookie dough onto sheet. Look at coals, which have gone to gray ash. Shiver. Close front flap of tent. Set cookies onto grill rack. Close stove. Put on a coat and hold hands on stove sides for warmth.

Wait as long as you can, until you think cookies are cooling inside stove, rather than warming. Remove tin sheet. Touch dough. Discover that, while not quite browned, dough is warmer than when put into stove.

Scrape cookie off sheet. Lean back in your chair, put your feet on table. Drop warm dough in mouth. Chew. Smile. Widen smile. Begin to ponder what you'll substitute for scallops when cooking Coquilles St. Jacques.

Serves one

Jodie's Famous Thai Shrimp

We first had this amazing dish when our friend Jodie, a fabulous cook, created it for us in our kitchen in Ketchum. It is also a wonderful way to serve sea bass, red snapper, or scallops. —C.G.

2 pounds raw medium shrimp, peeled and deveined
2 cups chicken broth
6–8 cloves garlic, minced
1 tablespoon finely minced fresh ginger
2–3 tablespoons Japanese mirin cooking wine
1–2 tablespoons soy sauce
2 tablespoons fresh Chinese chili paste or chili sauce
1–2 tablespoons cornstarch
1 cucumber, peeled, seeded, and thinly sliced
1/2 cup chopped fresh cilantro
1/2 cup chopped fresh green onions
2 limes, quartered

Combine chicken broth, garlic, ginger, cooking wine, soy sauce, and chili paste in a large bowl. Add the shrimp, cover, and marinate in the refrigerator for 1–2 hours.

Combine cornstarch with an equal amount cold water, and set aside.

Remove shrimp from the refrigerator, and pour off one quarter of the marinade. Place a large wok or skillet over the highest heat. When very hot, add the shrimp and marinade. Cook until the shrimp turn pink and feel firm to the touch. Lower heat. Stir in a little of the cornstarch mixture, and simmer, stirring frequently, until thickened. Serve at once over a platter of steamed rice or couscous, and sprinkle with the cucumber, cilantro, and green onions. Arrange lime quarters around the edges.

Serves 4

Carol and Scott Glenn

© 1991 Peter Kredenser

Scott Glenn is an unusual blend of sinewy adventurer and sensitive guy. He ice-climbs, sky-dives, and delivered his second daughter at home. He also loves to read poetry and cook. After meeting his wife-to-be on a blind date in 1967, Glenn pursued Carol to Paris, where she was working as a fashion model. They married a year later. The Glenns now live in Ketchum, Idaho, where Carol throws pots and paints, and he skis and enjoys the success of his films—*Silverado, The Right Stuff,* and *Silence of the Lambs,* to name a few. Truly concerned about his home state, Glenn has recorded radio spots opposing expansion of a bombing range in Idaho's Owyhee Desert, a high-mountain wilderness.

Only the mountain has lived long enough to listen objectively to the howl of a wolf.

Aldo Leopold—*A Sand County Almanac, with Other Essays on Conservation from Round River*

the howl

the wolf's howl has been called the most beautiful sound in the animal world— resonant and lingering, a seductive call, and the epitome of wildness. Wolves howl at any time during the day or night. Many situations and emotions precipitate this expression. Wolves howl to assemble the pack, to alert members of a threat near the den, and to locate each other in a storm or in unfamiliar territory. The pack howls when it is reunited after a hunt, possibly an expression of pleasure or excitement. Some Native American tribes believe that wolves howl after eating to summon ravens, fox, mice, coyotes, and other animals to pick the bones. During the winter, the time of courtship and mating, howling increases as the wolf serenades its mate with a jubilant invitation. On a calm night over open terrain, a howl can be heard up to 10 miles away. Wolves also howl to publicize their presence to a neighboring pack, declaring territorial boundaries. It seems they howl just because they like to. Whatever the reason, this primeval cry has gripped the human imagination, striking terror in days past and fascination today.

Lori McNee Watson ©95

territory

like man, the gray wolf is territorial. A wolf pack defends its territory to ensure that there is plentiful prey for the group and shelter for pups. A pack in Canada's far north may cover nearly 1,000 square miles, about the size of Rhode Island. In the Northern Rockies, a territory is usually about 300 square miles. Large enough to contain sufficient prey, the territory must also be small enough for the wolves to become familiar with every bend in the river.

The pack creates an invisible but powerful border around its territory by scent marking. At times, a wolf may lift his leg on rocks and trees every 400 yards. Revisiting these marks, the pack recognizes its home territory. The scent also warns intruding lone wolves or packs to stay away or face a challenge. Howling also cautions would-be trespassers to back off. In these ways, a pack patrols its frontier and protects its domain from marauders.

L. McNee Watson © 95

The thing that defines a wolf more than anything—better than DNA, better than fur, teeth, green eyes, better than even the low, mournful howl—is the way it travels. The home range of wolves in the northern Rockies averages 200 to 300 square miles, and ranges of 500 square miles are not uncommon. Montana could not be avoided by Canadian wolves. There are too many deer, too many elk: too many for the few predators that still exist.

—Rick Bass, *The Ninemile Wolves*

Al
Gore Jr.

Vice President Al Gore Jr. probably knows more about the ecology of this planet than any other man who has shared the White House. Gore is highly respected for his wide scope of environmental knowledge and command of complex issues. He understands the value of ecosystem management. In his book, *Earth in the Balance*, Gore states that lands should be managed within natural boundaries of mountain ranges and waterways rather than by political boundaries, as they are now managed.

Gore Family Spicy Stuffed Chicken

This is an exotic dish fit for a banquet with diplomats or that first dinner with that special someone. The sweet flavor of the parsnips plays off the garam masala, a Indian mixture of spices.

$3^{1}/_{2}$-pound roasting chicken
2 tablespoons olive oil
1 onion, finely diced
1 teaspoon garam masala
4 ounces button, brown, or chestnut mushrooms, coarsely chopped
1 cup coarsely grated parsnips
1 cup coarsely grated carrots
1 cup fresh white bread crumbs
1 egg, lightly beaten
$^{1}/_{4}$ cup chopped walnuts
2 teaspoons chopped fresh thyme, plus whole sprigs for garnish
salt and pepper to taste
1 tablespoon margarine
$^{2}/_{3}$ cup Marsala wine
watercress sprigs for garnish

Preheat oven to 375°.

In a large saucepan, heat olive oil and add onion. Sauté over medium heat for 5–10 minutes, or until softened. Stir in garam masala, and cook for 1 minute. Reduce heat to medium-low. Add mushrooms, parsnips, and carrots. Cook, stirring frequently, for 5 minutes. Remove from heat. Stir in bread crumbs, egg, walnuts, and chopped thyme. Add salt and pepper to taste, and set aside to cool completely.

Rinse chicken well, and pat dry with paper towels. Fill chicken with prepared stuffing, and truss it. Place chicken, breast down, in a roasting pan. Add $^{1}/_{4}$ cup water to the pan. Roast for 45 minutes, then turn breast up and dot with margarine. Roast 45 minutes more, or until a meat thermometer inserted in thickest part of thigh registers 185°. Transfer to a platter, and keep warm.

Pour off and discard fat from roasting pan. Add Marsala wine to remaining cooking juices, stirring to scrape up any browned bits. Bring to a boil over high heat, and cook for 1 minute to reduce slightly. Add salt and pepper to taste.

Remove skin from chicken and carve. Garnish sliced chicken with thyme and watercress sprigs. Serve with stuffing and flavored pan juices.

Serves 4

Howling Good Quacker

I shoot ducks. Lots! Have since I was ten. I developed this recipe after trying many others and it seemed to me to be the one my family and friends enjoyed the most. It's quick, easy, and really good. —J.G.

breasts of 1 duck
flour, salt, and pepper mixed together on a plate
butter or oil for sautéing
1/2 cup teriyaki sauce
1/2 cup each, or any combination, sliced water chestnuts, pineapple chunks, sliced red or green bell peppers, bamboo shoots, mushrooms, or any other favorite vegetables

Slice each breast piece into three or four 1/2-inch strips of meat. Dredge strips in the flour mixture.

Heat a little butter or oil in an large skillet, and lightly brown the duck strips. Pour off any remaining oil, and stir in teriyaki sauce.

Add the vegetables, cover the skillet, and steam to your liking. (Be careful not to overcook the duck; 15–20 minutes should suffice.) Serve over or next to a bed of brown or wild rice.

Serves 2

Jay Gore

Anything for wolves!

Wildlife biologist Jay Gore is described by his peers as a true leader, one who inspires others through his actions, motivating them to do their best. Employed by the federal government, Gore has also been a driving force for local activism in environmental protection. In 1986, Gore co-created the Wolf Recovery Foundation, in Boise, Idaho. Gore says, "If we can't make room for the survival of our fish and wildlife, we must not think much of ourselves." Now living in Ogden, Utah, Gore listens to rock 'n' roll and is the regional endangered species coordinator for the U.S. Forest Service.

Tipper Gore

Mary Elizabeth "Tipper" Gore relinquished her dream of becoming a child psychologist years ago and, instead, chose to concentrate on being a mother and wife. Indeed, she is the anchor of the Gore family—an involved, loving mother to her four children, and a supportive, playful wife to husband Al Gore Jr. She juggles her demanding schedule as a politician's spouse around her family, not vice versa. In 1987, Tipper was criticized for encouraging record companies to label music that had sexually explicit lyrics. Her crusade against the music industry's glamorization of sex and violence is now seen as ahead of its time.

Tennessee Treats

This is an irresistible lowfat recipe—it produces chewy, nutty little jewels with about as much effort as it takes to say "yes please." Be sure to make plenty—they go fast.

2 cups firmly packed dark brown sugar
4 eggs (2 whole eggs and 2 egg whites)
2 tablespoons honey
1 teaspoon baking powder
$^1/_4$ cup boiling water
2 cups all-purpose flour
$^1/_2$ teaspoon salt
$^1/_2$ teaspoon ground cinnamon
$^1/_8$ teaspoon ground allspice
$^1/_8$ teaspoon ground cloves
$^1/_2$ cup dates, chopped
$^1/_2$ cup raisins
$^1/_2$ cup walnut pieces

Preheat oven to 350°. Grease a 8x12-inch baking pan.

In a large mixing bowl, cream together brown sugar and eggs. Stir in honey and combine well. Add baking powder to the boiling water, and stir to dissolve. Pour this mixture into the mixing bowl.

In a separate medium bowl, combine flour, salt, and spices. Stir into mixing bowl. Fold in dates, raisins, and walnuts, and pour into prepared pan. Bake for 30–40 minutes. Treats are done when a toothpick inserted in the middle comes out nearly dry. Cut into 2x3-inch pieces while warm.

Makes 16 bars

Tipper Gore

Grandmother Mountain Wilderness Stuffed Bread

Great Old Broads for Wilderness would not dare to be too specific about ingredients for our cooking. We've been around long enough to know that you take what's there and make the best of it… then go out into the Wilderness… it has to be easy and portable. —S.T.

loaf (or loaves) French bread
butter (use lite and not much of it)
thinly sliced turkey breast
and/or
thinly sliced ham
oysters
and/or
steak
broccoli, chopped
fresh mushrooms, sliced
green onions, chopped
snow peas
or
whatever

Cut the top off the loaf (loaves) of bread about one-fourth of the way from the top. Scoop the insides out of both pieces.

Melt the butter. Using a pastry brush, brush the melted butter over both pieces of the bread. Line the bread pieces with the thinly sliced turkey (or ham, or whatever).

Sauté the oysters (steak, or whatever), the veggies, and "whatever" else, individually, in butter, cleaning the pan and using a fresh bit of butter with each "whatever." The juices should blend inside the bread.

After each item is sautéed, place onto the bread—thereby "stuffing" it. Place the top of the bread over the bottom. Wrap the stuffed loaf in foil, and either place into a warm oven for an hour, or refrigerate until needed. Once warm, remove foil and cut into 2-inch slices.

This then is our kind of recipe. You take whatever is available and desirable, whomp it together, wrap it, cool it or heat it, serve it, and take a hike!

Great Old Broads for Wilderness

Members of Great Old Broads for Wilderness resent politicians' claims that wilderness locks out the elderly. Faces wrinkled by years of sun, laughter, and life, President Susan Tixier and her GOB friends tramp up mountains, hike into desert canyons, and spend days in the backcountry, exploring the natural world. This granny grassroots group is fighting to preserve the country's remaining wilderness. GOBs have chained themselves to trees to halt logging and they have appeared before Congress, personally disputing the claim that only the young and strong benefit from wilderness.

Greater Yellowstone Coalition

With more than 10,000 geothermal features, free-roaming bison, staggering waterfalls, and expansive forests, the Greater Yellowstone Ecosystem is one of the most magical places on earth. At its core are Yellowstone and Grand Teton National Parks with surrounding public and private lands in Montana, Wyoming, and Idaho. The ecosystem's 18 million acres is home to the threatened grizzly bear, and endangered species, such as the bald eagle, trumpeter swan, and gray wolf. Formed in 1983, the Greater Yellowstone Coalition seeks to preserve the integrity of this wild corner by challenging logging, proposals for hydro-electric projects, hardrock mining, and other developments that would harm this fragile area.

Wild Ice Cream Pie

Chocolate, ice cream, whipping cream, and nuts = sheer bliss.

20 Oreo cookies
$1/3$ cup butter, melted
2 ounces unsweetened chocolate
2 tablespoons butter
$1/2$ cup sugar
5-ounce can evaporated milk
1 quart vanilla ice cream
1 cup heavy cream
2 tablespoons powdered sugar
2 tablespoons vanilla extract
$3/4$ cup chopped walnuts

Lightly butter a 9-inch springform pan. Crush cookies in a food processor. Pour in melted butter and mix. Press into prepared pan, and chill until firm.

In a medium saucepan, melt chocolate with butter over low heat. Stir in sugar, and combine well. Slowly pour in evaporated milk. Cook over medium-high heat for approximately 8 minutes, until thickened. Transfer to a bowl and chill, uncovered, in the refrigerator.

Thaw the ice cream slightly, then spread it into the pie shell, smoothing it evenly. Chill in the freezer until ice cream is firm. Spread with the chocolate sauce, and return to freezer.

Using an electric mixer, whip the cream with the powdered sugar and vanilla until it forms stiff peaks. Spread over pie, and sprinkle with chopped nuts. Freeze until firm, about 5 hours. Let stand at room temperature for 5 minutes before serving.

Serves 8

Wild Mushroom Risotto

Creamy Arborio rice readily absorbs the flavor of added ingredients. In this case, the strong, meat-like flavors of the wild mushrooms turn this into a fabulous meal.

1½ quarts (6 cups) chicken broth or stock
4 tablespoons olive oil
6 cups wild mushrooms (morels, porcini, chanterelles, or a mixture), wiped clean and sliced
2 cloves garlic, finely minced
salt and pepper to taste
1 medium yellow onion, finely chopped
1 small bunch fresh thyme, finely chopped (reserving a few sprigs)
1½ cups Arborio rice
1 cup dry white wine
4 tablespoons unsalted butter
chopped fresh parsley for garnish

Place chicken stock in a 2-quart saucepan, and bring to a simmer over low heat.

Heat 2 tablespoons of the olive oil in a large skillet. Add mushrooms and garlic. Sauté until the mushrooms release moisture, about 5 minutes. Salt and pepper the mushrooms, and set aside.

Heat remaining 2 tablespoons of olive oil in a large saucepan. Add onion and the sprigs of thyme. Sauté over medium heat until onions are translucent, about 7–10 minutes. Add rice, and stir constantly for 2–3 minutes. Stir in the wine, and cook until it's almost evaporated.

Pour in 1 cup of the warmed chicken stock. As the rice begins to absorb it, continue adding the stock in ½-cup increments over the next 15 minutes. Stir often, keeping the rice moist.

Raise the heat, add the mushrooms, and bring to a boil. Lower the heat so that the rice is at a simmer. Continue adding the remaining stock, ½ cup at a time, stirring constantly, until the rice is slightly creamy and just tender. Taste frequently to check the progress of the rice. Altogether the rice should cook for 25–35 minutes, until the mixture is creamy and rice is al denté.

When the rice is almost done, stir in the butter. Add salt and pepper to taste. Stir in the chopped fresh parsley and thyme, and serve immediately.

Serves 4

Paul Hawken

Businessmen like Paul Hawken may be as rare as endangered species. The cofounder of Smith & Hawken, a premier garden catalog company, believes that commerce and environmental ethics are not only compatible but necessary. In fact, Hawken writes in *The Ecology of Commerce* that with natural resources becoming increasingly limited, industrialism is verging on collapse. America must switch from a growth economy to a restorative one, he says, in which businesses are rewarded for conserving resources and avoiding environmental harm. Hawken and his wife, Anna, live in Sausalito, California.

Charles H. Hayes

Nez Perce Tribal Chairman Charles Hayes knows the importance of keeping the wolf in the world. "It is up to us to live within the bounds that our Mother Earth has given us. If we don't, sooner or later Mother Earth takes back what was always hers in the first place." The tribe will soon have wolves living among them. The Nez Perce, descendants of Chief Joseph, live near Lewiston, Idaho. Their homeland is the site of the Wolf Education and Research Center's 20-acre enclosure and interpretive trail system for observation of the Sawtooth Wolf Pack. Hayes says, "The tribe looks forward to meeting our brother, the wolf, at the ancient spiritual sites of our ancestors. Once again we'll be able to talk and listen to his stories of survival which connect us to our past and which will help lead us into our future."

Saddle Blankets

This recipe evokes images of a crystal-clear western dawn, and the tempting aroma of sizzling bacon, coffee, and sweet maple syrup.

3 cups flour
$^1/_4$ cup sugar
2 teaspoons baking powder
1 teaspoon salt
2 cups milk
1 egg, lightly beaten
2 tablespoons butter, melted, or oil
1 cup fresh huckleberries or blueberries, if available

Sift the flour into a large mixing bowl, and add sugar, baking powder, and salt. Add milk, egg, and oil, and stir to combine. Gently fold in the huckleberries.

Lightly oil and heat a large griddle or skillet. Pour batter onto hot griddle to form 5-inch rounds. Turn pancakes only once, and serve hot with maple syrup or jam. (A handful of cornmeal may be added to the batter to provide for a browner saddle blanket and a little flavor variation.)

Makes 24 pancakes

Bad Dog Fettuccine

I stole this recipe (rather I recreated it as best I could) from the now-defunct restaurant Norris in Columbus, Ohio. It was one of the things I missed the most about Ohio when I returned, after a year of teaching, to my home in the West. —P.H.

2 tablespoons olive oil
1 large red onion, slivered
3 medium jalapeño peppers, seeded and diced
2 cups sweet corn
2 cloves garlic, minced
3 tablespoons chopped fresh rosemary
1½ cups heavy cream
1 pound fresh red pepper fettuccine
salt and freshly ground black pepper to taste

Heat olive oil in a large saucepan. Add onion, peppers, corn, garlic, and rosemary. Sauté over medium heat until the onion is soft, about 10 minutes. Add cream, and cook just under the boiling point, until the cream starts to thicken, about 5 minutes (double the cooking time in high altitudes).

Bring a large pot of salted water to a boil, and add the pasta. Cook at a rolling boil until just tender. Drain pasta, toss together with the sauce, and season with salt and pepper. Serve in a large, heated pasta bowl.

Serves 4

Pam Houston

Steve Griffin

In Pam Houston's best selling first book, *Cowboys Are My Weakness,* the female characters all have a serious case of bad taste in men. These strong and smart women know they should know better, but they don't. They follow their cowboys, a group of unpredictable, and untamable men to the end of the earth. The resulting conflict gives a new twist to the age old sexual politic. A character herself, Houston also has a weakness for adventure. She likes to ski extreme terrain, avalanche chutes and waist-deep powder, although she says she is only an advanced-intermediate skier. She has a weakness for the West—a part of the country, she says, she should have been born in, had not some cosmic joke landed her in New Jersey.

International Wolf Center

International Wolf Center

Located near Ely, Minnesota, in the Boundary Waters Canoe Area, the International Wolf Center sits at the heart of the largest wolf population in the Lower 48 states. Visitors learn about the natural history of wolves on evening howling adventures, snowshoeing to kill sites, flying over wolf territory, observing the Center's captive pack, and touring the award-winning "Wolves and Humans" exhibit. Scientists from around the world meet there frequently to share research, making the Center a focal point for international environmental education.

Hunter's Sauce

This marvelous recipe is contributed by Jim Orcutt and Jon Benson, the chefs and owners of The Chocolate Moose Restaurant in Ely, Minnesota, in cooperation with the International Wolf Center. It is an excellent sauce for wild game, but also can be used on chicken, beef, or pork.

5 slices smoked bacon, diced
$^1/_8$ cup minced onion or 2 small shallots, minced
1 large clove garlic, minced
$^1/_3$ cup wild mushrooms (shiitake, morels, or oyster), sliced
$^1/_3$ cup white button mushrooms, sliced
$^1/_2$ cup Burgundy wine
$^1/_2$ teaspoon each of rosemary, thyme, sage, and parsley (if using fresh, use 1 teaspoon each)
1 medium tomato, diced
3 green onions, diced
$1^1/_2$ cups veal or beef stock
roux (equal parts melted butter and flour cooked for 5 minutes)
salt and pepper to taste

In a large skillet, sauté bacon over medium heat until it starts to brown. Add the onion or shallots, garlic, and mushrooms, stirring occasionally until mushrooms start to brown.

Add the Burgundy and herbs, and simmer until the liquid is reduced by half. Add the tomato, green onions, and stock, and bring to a boil. Reduce the heat, and simmer for 2–3 minutes.

Stir in a small amount of roux, and cook for 2–3 minutes more. (Sauce should be medium-thick, and can be adjusted by adding more Burgundy to thin or roux to thicken.) Season with salt and pepper. Pour sauce over wild game or other freshly cooked meats.

Serves 4–6

Jack London's Roast Duck

This recipe was contributed in 1915 by Jack London to The Suffrage Cookbook. *Milo Shepard, a descendant of Jack London, provided us with a copy. It is a timeless version of the perfect roast duck.*

1 wild duck, oven-ready
¹/₂ cup chopped celery
salt and pepper
juice of 1 lemon
paprika

The only way in the world to serve a canvas-back or a mallard, or a sprig, or even the toothsome teal, is as follows:

The plucked bird should be stuffed with a tight handful of plain raw celery and, in a piping oven, roasted variously 8, 9, 10, or even 11 minutes, according to size of bird and heat of oven.

The blood-rare breast is carved with the leg and carcass, then thoroughly squeezed in a press. The resultant liquid is seasoned with salt, pepper, lemon, and paprika, and poured hot over the meat.

This method of roasting insures the maximum tenderness and flavor in the bird. The longer the wild duck is roasted, the dryer and tougher it becomes.

Serves 2

Jack London Vineyard

Robert Nixon

In 1905, author Jack London began buying broken-down ranches in the Sonoma Valley. Nine years later, he had purchased a total of seven and turned them into one holding of more than 1,300 acres. After London's death in 1916, about 1,000 acres were given to the state of California for the Jack London State Park. Milo Shepard, a descendant of London's, manages the remaining vineyards. London delighted in being called by his nickname Wolf and was obsessed with the predator. His classics, *Call of the Wild* and *White Fang*, remain immensely popular.

Mike Jimenez

After biologist Mike Jimenez found five hungry orphaned wolf pups in Montana's Ninemile Valley, he began to peel flattened animals from the highway and left the road kill near the den. The wild pups took to the dead game and soon he had a supply problem. Jimenez put word out in the close-knit rural community. Bikers, bus drivers, school children, and ranchers began calling Jimenez when they saw fresh kill on the roadside. In response, he drove at all hours, in all conditions, over many miles collecting the meat before other scavengers claimed it. He continued to feed the pups in this way until they surprised Jimenez by stalking their first prey.

Nancy Seldin's All-Weather Twice-Cooked Bread

Nancy Seldin makes this "field food" for her husband, Mike. The twice-baked sweet bread won't freeze in sub-zero temperatures, and it is packed with nutrients and calories, important for a wiry guy like Mike.

2 eggs
1 cup canola oil
2 cups firmly packed brown sugar
4 teaspoons vanilla extract
2 cups unbleached all-purpose flour
1/2 cup rice polish (available at health-food stores)
8 teaspoons soy flour
8 teaspoons wheat germ
8 teaspoons skim-milk powder
2 teaspoons baking soda
1 teaspoon each: ground nutmeg, cloves, cinnamon, and allspice, to taste
1/2 teaspoon baking powder
2 cups shredded zucchini and/or carrots (depending on supply)
4 cups chopped dried fruit (raisins, apples, apricots, currants)

Preheat oven to 325°. Butter and flour two 9x5x3-inch loaf pans.

In a large bowl, mix together the eggs, canola oil, brown sugar, and vanilla until well blended. Set aside.

In a separate large bowl, mix together the dry ingredients. Add this mixture to the egg mixture, and blend well. Stir in the vegetables and fruits, stirring as little as possible to blend.

Spoon into prepared pans, using a rubber spatula. Bake for approximately 60–70 minutes, or until a toothpick inserted in the center of a loaf comes out clean.

Allow to cool on wire racks. Once loaves are completely cooled (or several days later), slice loaves into 1/2-inch slices. Arrange these on baking racks in the oven. Leave slices in oven overnight on the lowest setting (in our oven that's approximately 150°). Cool, and cover with plastic wrap, or place in Ziploc bags. (If you collect wolf scat, we'd suggest using different-sized baggies so there's no confusion as to what's what!)

Makes 2 loaves

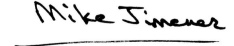

Chilean Sea Bass

Maui onions lend a sweet contrast to the acerbic flavor of the tomato sauce. This easy-to-prepare plate is great for company with its red, white, and gold presentation.

6 Maui or other large sweet onions, sliced
6 tablespoons unsalted butter
12 Roma tomatoes, seeded and chopped
5 shallots, chopped
3 cloves garlic, chopped
1/2 cup chopped fresh basil
1 tablespoon extra virgin olive oil
1/2 cup chicken broth
2 pounds Chilean sea bass, in thick pieces
salt
white pepper

Preheat oven to 425°.

In a large skillet, sauté onions with butter over medium-low heat until caramelized (about 30 minutes).

Using a food processor, puree the tomatoes, shallots, garlic, and basil.

Heat olive oil in a large saucepan. Add pureed ingredients, and cook over low heat for 15–20 minutes. Add chicken broth as needed to maintain liquid consistency. Keep sauce warm.

Place fish in a baking dish, and season with salt and white pepper to taste. Cover with onions, and bake for 10–12 minutes. Spoon sauce on warm plates, and place 1 serving of fish on top of sauce.

Serves 4

James Earl Jones

James Earl Jones grew up in rural Mississippi listening to the cadence of Southern voices. When he was ten, his family moved to Michigan and that trauma triggered a stuttering problem that would last four years. Today, Jones is recognized throughout the world for his unmistakable deep voice—he was Darth Vader in the *Star Wars* trilogy and *The Lion King*'s Mufasa—and his tremendous acting talent—he starred in *Clear and Present Danger* and *A Family Thing*. Jones says he finds a safe haven and a soothing connection to nature at his farm in upstate New York, where he lives with his wife, actress Cecelia Hart, and their son Flynn.

Donna Karan

Donna Karan is the only woman in the male world of Seventh Avenue's top fashion designers. Karan makes wearable, flattering clothes for real women, whether they are corporate lawyers, Candice Bergen, or doctors' wives. A creative genius, she is also a formidable businesswoman with a fortune amassed in the hundreds of millions of dollars. Karan is a strong supporter of AIDS research and other charitable causes. The ever-restless Karan works too hard in the city to spend much time at her beach house in East Hampton.

Designer Chicken Soup

A real all-American soup. When the weather turns raw, there's nothing like a lovely, big pot of soul-satisfying chicken soup simmering on the stove. Add a basket of Linda Ronstadt's buttered corn muffins for an even more impressive feast.

4 pounds skinless free-range chicken, cut into 8 pieces
4 chicken wings
3 celery stalks, cut in half crosswise
3 carrots, peeled and cut into $1/2$-inch slices
1 turnip, peeled and halved
1 parsnip, peeled and halved
1 sweet yellow onion, halved (Vidalia, Maui, or Walla Walla, if available)
1 bunch fresh dill, chopped, reserving a little for garnish
1 bunch fresh parsley, chopped
1 tablespoon Vogue brand organic chicken stock powder
1 tablespoon Vogue brand organic vegetable stock powder
1 teaspoon salt
6 black peppercorns
4 quarts water
thinly sliced boiled carrots for garnish

Place all ingredients (except those for garnish) in a large stock pot. Bring to a boil, reduce heat, and simmer for 3 hours, partially covering the pot with the lid. Add water if necessary to keep chicken and vegetables covered.

Remove soup from heat, and allow it to cool to room temperature. Place in refrigerator and chill overnight.

Skim fat off the top, and discard. Remove the meat from the chicken pieces, and set it aside. Discard the bones and skin. Strain the soup twice, and discard the vegetables.

Add the chicken meat to the strained broth, along with the boiled carrots and dill. Reheat, and ladle into large soup bowls.

Serves 8

Jack London Cabernet Peppercorn Sauce

Kenwood Vineyards

We strive to use our wines in our weekend food and wine program at the winery. Every June at Kenwood Vineyards is Jack London month. This sauce was developed to go with our Cabernet Sauvignon, made from grapes grown at the Jack London Vineyard. It is intended to go over grilled London broil, but can also be used as a marinade and a basting sauce for other grilled meats, chicken, or vegetables. —Winery chef Carlo DiClemente

¹/₄ cup mixed whole peppercorns (a combination of black, white, green, pink, and red)
¹/₄ cup Kenwood Jack London Cabernet Sauvignon
1 tablespoon sweet-hot mustard
1 tablespoon balsamic vinegar
¹/₂ cup extra virgin olive oil

Using a spice grinder, or a mortar and pestle, grind the peppercorns and set aside.

Pour the Cabernet Sauvignon into a small sauté pan, and bring to a slight boil over low heat. Simmer until wine is reduced to 1 tablespoon.

Place the peppercorns, reduced wine, mustard, and vinegar in a food processor. Blend together, and, with the motor running, slowly drizzle the olive oil through the feed tube. Continue to process until sauce is thickened, about 1–2 minutes. Ladle sauce over meat, or refrigerate until ready to use. (Sauce will separate if it gets too warm.)

Serves 2

California's Kenwood Vineyards produces wolf lovers' favorite wine: the Jack London Vineyard Cabernet Sauvignon. This wine has its own identifiable character, hearty black currant inside and a noble wolf face painted on the dark bottle. The winery sits in the Sonoma Valley—what the Miwok Indians called the Valley of the Moons, as the moon seems to rise several times each evening, appearing among the mountain peaks to the east.

Carole King

When Carole King spoke before Congress in support of the Northern Rockies Ecosystem Protection Act, she earned respect from both sides of the controversy for her insightful comments and command of the issue. In the late 1970s, King exited the fast lane because she wanted peace of mind and to live a more natural lifestyle. Since coming to Idaho, King has moved several times around the state, each time to a more remote area. The Grammy-winning singer and songwriter, best remembered for her classic album *Tapestry*, now lives on a ranch on a tributary of Idaho's Salmon River.

Salmon River Pasta with Lentil Sauce

This lusty dish has a rich, nutty flavor and is nearly fat-free.
Use a robust pasta such rotelle, fusilli, or penne.

2 3/4 cups water
1 cup dried lentils
2/3 cup dried split peas
2 tablespoons vegetable oil
1 onion, finely chopped
1 clove garlic, crushed
1 carrot, finely chopped
1 celery stalk, finely chopped
15-ounce can tomatoes, drained and chopped
1 teaspoon dried oregano
salt and pepper to taste
1 pound dried pasta

In a medium saucepan, bring water to a boil. Stir in lentils and split peas. Simmer, covered, for about 40 minutes, or until all liquid has been absorbed and lentils and peas are soft. Set aside.

Heat oil in a separate medium saucepan. Add onion, garlic, carrot, and celery. Sauté over low heat, stirring occasionally, until soft. Stir in tomatoes and oregano, and season with salt and pepper. Cover pan, and simmer gently for 5 minutes. Meanwhile, prepare pasta according to directions on package.

Add cooked lentils and peas to vegetable mixture. Cook, stirring occasionally, until well combined and heated through. Ladle over pasta.

Serves 4–6

Enchiladas de Queso y Pollo

*Manager Wally Hanly sends us this traditional dish,
from the Gulf of Mexico, on behalf of Los Lobos. These are extremely good,
and despite all the chiles, not too hot.*

Sauce:
6 cups water
6-ounce can tomato paste
¹⁄₄ cup ground dried New Mexico or red poblano (ancho) chiles
(remove and discard seeds and grind in a food processor)
8 ounces grated blend of Monterey Jack and Cheddar cheese
1 tablespoon Worcestershire sauce
¹⁄₂ teaspoon paprika (optional)
¹⁄₄ teaspoon oregano
salt to taste
white pepper to taste

Chicken:
4 pounds chicken, cut into pieces
1 yellow onion, chopped
2 carrots, sliced
4 whole cloves garlic, peeled
¹⁄₄ cup chopped fresh parsley
1 small piece of fresh ginger (1 inch), peeled and sliced
¹⁄₄ cup dry sherry
1 teaspoon dried thyme
1 teaspoon dried oregano
1 teaspoon black pepper

Filling:
8 ounces grated Monterey Jack cheese, reserving 1 ounce
3.8-ounce can chopped black olives, drained
1 yellow onion, very finely chopped
3 cups of the shredded chicken (from above)

1 dozen corn tortillas
3 chopped green onions
1 cup shredded lettuce

To prepare the sauce: In a large saucepan, bring the water to a boil and stir in tomato paste. After it dissolves, add the rest of the sauce ingredients. Boil gently, uncovered, for 30 minutes, or until sauce thickens. Use a little masa harina or cornstarch to thicken if necessary. The sauce will improve if refrigerated, and will keep up to 3 days.

Los Lobos

Dennis Keeley

The Grammy-winning Los Lobos (Spanish for "The Wolves") has retained its original vision and members since its beginning in 1973. The quintet first began playing what drummer Louie Perez calls "the soundtrack of the Barrio." They performed at Cinco de Mayo parties, VFW and American Legion Halls... anywhere in their native East L.A., where people congregated to hear rock, roadhouse blues, and those rich, pure strains straight from the Mexican heartland. In their 1984 debut album, *How Will the Wolf Survive?*, the wolf represents the question of whether traditional values will survive in a changing world. Los Lobos is still Perez, Steve Berlin, David Hidalgo, Conrad Lozano, and Cesar Rosas.

To prepare the chicken and broth: Place chicken in a large stock pot. Cover with water, add all chicken ingredients, and bring to a boil. Reduce heat, and simmer for 1½ hours. Turn off heat. Remove chicken from broth and allow to cool. Save the broth. When chicken is cool, remove the skin and bones, and shred the chicken meat into small pieces. Place the skin and bones back into the broth, and simmer for another hour. Cool and strain the broth, and place it in a large saucepan.

To make the filling: Combine Monterey Jack cheese, olives, onion, and chicken in a medium bowl.

Preheat oven to 325°. Lightly grease a 9x13-inch casserole.

To assemble: Warm the sauce and the chicken broth both to just above room temperature. Set up an "assembly line", starting with the chicken broth, the red sauce, the baking dish, and then the filling. Using tongs, dip 1 tortilla into the broth, remove, and let drip for a moment. Dip it into the red sauce, and place in the baking dish. Spread ½ cup filling into the tortilla, roll it tight, and arrange in the pan, seam side down. Repeat this procedure with the remaining tortillas. Pour 1 cup (or more) of the red sauce over the enchiladas and sprinkle with the reserved cheese. Place in oven for 10–12 minutes, or until the cheese melts. Garnish with green onions and lettuce, and serve at once.

Serves 6

Mimi's Pound Cake

*Andie has many fond childhood memories of this pound cake
baked by her grandmother.*

1 cup (2 sticks) butter, softened
2 cups sugar
4 eggs
3 cups flour
$^1/_2$ teaspoon baking soda
$^1/_4$ teaspoon salt
$^1/_2$ cup milk
1 teaspoon vanilla extract
1 teaspoon cream of tartar

Preheat oven to 350°. Butter and flour a 9x5x3-inch loaf pan. Have all ingredients at room temperature.

In a large bowl, cream together butter and sugar with an electric mixer until light and fluffy. Separate egg yolks from the whites, and set the whites aside. Beat yolks, and add to creamed mixture. Blend until lemon colored.

Sift together flour, baking soda, and salt. Add to above, mixing until thoroughly blended. Beat in milk and vanilla.

In a separate bowl, beat whites with cream of tartar until they hold soft peaks. Fold them gently into the cake batter. Pour the batter into the prepared pan, and bake for 1 hour. The edges of the cake should begin to pull away from the sides of the pan when done. Cool on a rack for 15 minutes. Loosen the sides gently with a spatula, and invert the cake onto the rack to finish cooling. Slice, and serve it plain, with fresh fruit, or with a dusting of powdered sugar.

Serves 8

Andie MacDowell

Rosalie Anderson MacDowell finds sanity among the wolves on her 2,500-acre ranch tucked between the Rattlesnake and Bitterroot Ranges of isolated western Montana. She thinks modestly of herself as a "mother who has a pretty good acting career." In 1989, *sex, lies and videotape* launched then-megamodel MacDowell into stardom. *Four Weddings and a Funeral* cinched what continues to be a pretty darn good acting career. This South Carolina belle has chosen to raise her children on one of the few sites in the Northern Rockies where wolves choose to den. From their log cabin, built by her husband, ex-model Paul Qualley, the family can see wolf pups jaw-wrestle and play tag.

Shirley MacLaine

Dancing, in many ways, defines Shirley MacLaine. Thriving on screen and stage for more than four decades, she has waltzed her way through a choice array of prime films, including the Oscar-winning *Terms of Endearment.* In her life's dance, she has been a political activist, delegate for Robert Kennedy and George McGovern, and a champion of many humanistic causes. She glides effortlessly from acting to writing bestsellers about spiritual quests. And then, there are those legs. MacLaine owns a home in Malibu and the Plaza Blanca Ranch, 7,357 acres near Abiquiu, New Mexico, where her life slows down and she finds time to write.

Shirley MacLaine's Favorite Chicken Mushroom Soup

Sure to cure whatever ails you, this simple chicken soup is enhanced by the superb flavor of fresh mushrooms.

3 pounds chicken, whole or quartered, rinsed
1¹/₂ tablespoons vegetable or olive oil
1 clove garlic, crushed
1 teaspoon ground coriander
1 teaspoon ground peppercorns
4 ounces fresh mushrooms, sliced
1 teaspoon soy sauce
salt to taste

Place chicken and giblets in a large stock pot and cover with cold water. Bring to a boil, lower the heat, and skim the surface. Simmer for 1 hour uncovered. Add water if needed to maintain level in pot.

Remove meat from bones and cut into small pieces. Place bones back into the stock, and simmer for 2 more hours. Strain stock into a separate bowl and reserve. (Remove chicken livers from the giblets, chop, and set aside.)

Using the large stock pot, heat oil over medium-low heat. Add garlic, coriander, and peppercorns, and sauté for 1 minute. Stir in mushrooms and chicken meat (including the liver). Sauté for 3 minutes, then add 4 cups of the stock. Increase heat to medium-high, and simmer for 5 minutes. Add soy sauce, stir well, and season with salt. Ladle into bowls and serve at once.

Serves 4

Aubergine Caponata

This dish is best chilled for twenty-four hours before serving.
Serve with pasta or rice, and a salad. —L.M.

1 large aubergine (eggplant)
1 small onion
1 celery stalk
1 ounce olives
1 tablespoon capers
2¹/₂ tablespoons olive oil
1 tablespoon chopped fresh parsley
1 tablespoon wine vinegar
2 teaspoons sugar
1 cup chopped tomatoes
1 tablespoon tomato puree
salt and pepper to taste

Dice the aubergine into small cubes and sprinkle generously with salt. Leave on a plate for about 20 minutes to draw out the bitterness.

While the aubergine is standing, prepare the rest of the ingredients. Chop the onion, celery, olives, and capers into small pieces.

Heat the olive oil in a deep frying pan, and sauté the onion and celery for about 5 minutes, until lightly browned. Wash the salted aubergine thoroughly, drain, and add to the sauté, a few cubes at a time so the pieces do not absorb too much oil. Add more oil if necessary.

Add the remaining ingredients. Cover the pan and simmer over low-to-medium heat, stirring frequently, for 30 minutes. Chill.

Serves 8–10

Linda McCartney

Despite their superstar status, Linda McCartney and her husband, Paul, have adopted a quiet, unaffected lifestyle based out of their country home in Berkshire, England. McCartney grows herbs and vegetables and raises sheep for wool. A lifelong animal lover, McCartney became a vegetarian more than twenty-five years ago. In a moment of truth, she decided to forgo the leg of lamb on her plate when she noticed the sight of their farm sheep gamboling outside. McCartney has been a photojournalist, keyboard player in her husband's band, fashion designer, and best-selling cookbook author.

Denali Five-Minute Pasta

Rick McIntyre

Clark Mishler

Rick McIntyre's *A Society of Wolves: National Parks and the Battle Over the Wolf* and its sequel *The War Against the Wolf: America's Campaign to Exterminate the Wolf* are two of the most important books any wolf fan could own. They document the past attitudes and events that have led the wolf toward extinction. McIntyre has worked as a park ranger for more than twenty years in such revered places as Yellowstone, Denali, Glacier, Big Bend, and Sequoia National Parks. He is also a wildlife photographer and has an impressive collection of wild wolf photographs, taken during his years at Denali and Yellowstone.

During the years I lived in Alaska, I often spent long days out on the tundra watching wolves as they hunted, played with their pups, and relaxed. At the end of the day, I was very hungry and wanted to eat the moment I got home. Having little tolerance for time-consuming preparation, I figured out a way of cooking a great-tasting pasta dinner in under five minutes. This quick dinner gave me plenty of time to write up my wolf observations in my journal and get to bed early enough so that I could get up the next morning at 5 A.M. for another day of wolf watching. —R.M.

1/2 pound ground turkey or chicken
1/2 pound angel hair or spaghetti
2 cups (26 ounces) spaghetti sauce
herbs to taste: basil, oregano, thyme, parsley
2 tablespoons butter
freshly grated Parmesan cheese

Bring a large pot of salted water to a boil.

Using a medium skillet, cook the ground turkey or chicken over medium-high heat. Drain meat, and stir in the spaghetti sauce and herbs. Simmer over low heat.

Cook the angel hair according to directions, and drain. Place it back into the pot, and toss with the butter. Place the pasta on a heated plate, and ladle the sauce over it. Sprinkle with Parmesan cheese, and serve immediately.

Serves 1–2

Isle Royale Marinated Beef

This couldn't-be-simpler recipe can easily be made with other meats such as pork or chicken. If you use pork, substitute apple cider instead of wine in the marinade, and add fresh apple chunks to the onions and mushrooms.

1 flank or skirt steak (2–2^1/$_2$ pounds), cut into ^{1}/$_4$-inch slices
2 medium onions, finely chopped
^{1}/$_2$ pound (2^1/$_2$ cups) mushrooms, thinly sliced
3–4 tablespoons olive or canola oil

Marinade:
1 cup red wine
1 cup soy sauce
1 cup vinegar

Whisk together marinade, and set aside.

Place beef slices, onions, and mushrooms in a bowl large enough to hold all ingredients, and pour the marinade over. Marinate 1–2 hours (the longer the better).

Heat the oil in a heavy skillet. Remove the beef and vegetables from the marinade with a slotted spoon, and place them in the skillet. Reserve the marinade. Sauté the beef and vegetables, stirring occasionally, for 10–15 minutes.

Dilute the reserved marinade with 1^1/$_2$ cups of water. Add 2–3 cups of this mixture to the meat and vegetables, and continue cooking for 10 minutes, or until heated through. (The amount of marinade added depends on how much sauce is desired.) Ladle over cooked wild rice, noodles, or potatoes.

Note: This recipe can be increased easily. Just keep marinade portions in equal thirds.

Serves 4

L. David Mech

The world's preeminent living authority on wolves, biologist L. David Mech has spent years flying in rickety old aircraft, withstanding deep-freeze temperatures, and fighting flies at Isle Royale in Lake Superior, Alaska, and the Canadian Arctic. He understands the smallest details of the wolf's life and his findings have given us the most comprehensive picture of the species. Mech is a man of paradoxes. Field research is his passion. It is usually conducted in isolated locations under the most primitive living conditions. But when in the city, Mech trades his big fur hat and checkered wool jacket for a suit coat and a night at the opera. Puccini's *Turandot* is his favorite.

a year with the sawtooth pack in idaho's backcountry **megan parker on wolf camp**

Kathy Maechtle

Strapping my belongings—a futon, skis, candles, clothes, and other essentials—onto the back of a four-wheeler, I moved to Wolf Camp. I would spend the next year caretaking the camp located at the foot of Idaho's Sawtooth Mountains and conducting research on the five members of the Sawtooth Wolf Pack.

On that premier April morning, I drove the four-wheeler along a rutted trail to Wolf Camp. The nearest town, Stanley, population 71, is four miles away. In the winter, the dirt road leading to town would be covered by five feet of snow and I frequently cross-country skied the distance for supplies and conversation. I am used to isolation, having spent the past 3 years studying birds in the everglade marshes of Florida and the rainforest of Guatemala. It was great to be back in the Northern Rockies. As a native Montanan, I felt the familiar pull that spring morning of clean air, jagged granite mountains, and endless sky. I knew I was home.

I took this job, in part, because I knew it would be a terrific opportunity for a research biologist to observe and study wolves. We still know relatively little about this intelligent predator. My research focuses on how an individual wolf can be identified by its recorded voice print, just as human fingerprints are distinctive. I hope to expand my research so that it can be applied to wild wolves. In the future, we may be able to identify and track wolves by recording their voice prints and, in some cases, eliminate the need to anesthetize and track them with expensive radio collars.

The Sawtooth Pack, born in captivity, is accustomed to people, yet as with all wild animals they remain unpredictable. Within their 20-acre enclosure, the pack behaves, in many ways, like wolves in the wild. They howl, play, mark their territory, and keep social order through displays of dominance and submission. The enclosure is the largest in the United States and that expanse gives the pack room to play actively, run full-out, and find solitude.

While at Wolf Camp, my ten-year-old Dutch shepard, Marley, and I made our home in a 16-foot diameter yurt. Living in this western version of a Mongolian nomad's tent had its disadvantages—a cold plywood floor, uninvited four-footed guests, no running water, no electricity, and few modern conveniences. It was a remarkable life. At an elevation of 6,300 feet, the yurt's skylight opened up to a Milky Way almost too bright and close to be comprehensible. My life was filled with work and research at camp, and camp was filled with wildlife. Black bears wondered through, coyotes left tracks on my porch, and elk bugled in the forest during the autumn months.

I have come away from Wolf Camp with a better understanding of and deep respect for this species. I hope my field notes provide some insight into this evolved and complex society.

APRIL 30   My first day alone with the pack. I approached them kneeling so that they could easily obtain whatever information wolves get from licking and smelling the face of a newcomer. Kamots, the alpha, was first to greet me, followed by the rest. They mobbed me, tugging at my ponytail, coat and boots. If I had been standing, they would have knocked me down. They were testing me with their frenetic and insistent attention. More than 120 pounds of wolf multiplied by five left me feeling somewhere between disconcerted and afraid. I wondered if they remembered my smell from the other times I had met them. Was my olfactory imprint stored in their memory? Fact. A wolf's sense of smell is incredibly sensitive. Where a friend may recognize the single strong smell of my Aveda shampoo, the wolves are likely to pick up hundreds of scents from me.

MAY 4   The pack is beginning to shed. They were panting today in their thick winter coats which have stood them in minus 50 degree weather. In a frenzy, they scratched out huge tufts of undercoat, rolled in the grass and shook to free themselves of the stifling fur.

As they shed, their heads and bodies become more defined, sleek and lanky. They look more wild somehow than they did when their features were concealed by their massive coats. Their legs seem impossibly long. They're built to travel. I looked at Kamots today with new

gained respect. His head is broader than the span of a man's large hand. His jaw musculature is tremendous. The muscles of the mandible are attached to the now-prominent sagital crest at the top of his scull. In this new lean package, his eyes are even more intense.

JUNE 20 I followed the wolves up the slope above the aspen grove. The morning mist collected above the mossy area surrounding the cold water spring and obscured them at first. I could barely make out their silhouettes. Soon, I realized they were grazing on shooting stars. I was stunned to see wolves devouring wild flowers but this pack plucked and ate bouquet after bouquet.

This afternoon, Marley and I walked back to camp after buying groceries in Stanley. We found eight sets of deep, dumb eyes gazing back at us. The neighboring rancher's cows had broken through the fence and were placidly eating the grass around the yurt. They had already lunched their way through my garden. They ate the pitiful lettuce, spinach, garlic and herbs that I had been nursing along for two months, carrying water from the creek, and covering when temperatures dropped into the teens.

JULY 3 The pups are here! They are three silky-furred, perpetual motion machines that are as curious as their world will allow them to be. They explore the long grass, trees, creek, fallen logs and pine cones of their quarter-acre enclosure. For a short time the pups are being held adjacent to the adults, until they are old enough to join the pack and both sides get used to one another. There is much watching, yipping, staring, barking, howling and whining back and forth. They sniff at the air currents, catching downwind scents from other wolves. Undoubtedly, there is an entire vocabulary of scent I am unaware of.

JULY 20 Jim Dutcher and his crew are here to film the pups as they enter the larger world of the pack. They greeted Jim with anxious yelping, instantly recognizing their surrogate father, the man who had raised them. All the wolves are very comfortable with Jim and his crew and camera equipment. It's thrilling to witness and be a part of the sequel to Wolf: Return of a Legend.

94

The bond that the pups and adults have formed with Jim created a cohesive bridge for this introduction to go very smoothly. The pups belly-crawl out of their pen, instantly submitting to the larger wolves. It was a tense moment as Kamots towered over them but he quickly turned the mood toward play and acceptance.

SEPTEMBER 22   Today was much like the Indian summers I know from Montana. The sun warmed the day but when it fell behind Williams Peak, I was suddenly reminded of the piercing cold to come. Until today, I have peacefully co-existed with the mice; they spent most of their time outdoors. But they have also been reminded of winter's coming and have invaded my yurt in legions along with 10, 20, or maybe 200 chipmunks. Everyone is looking for a snug place to wait out winter. I found dried dog food cached in my long underwear this morning and when I lit my oven to bake bread, I smelled that mice were living there. The chipmunks are brazen and chirr at me when they get a chance, seeming to resent my taking up so much space in the crowded yurt. The live traps I set are a joke to these survivalist-trained rodents. Marley, side, seems to consider

who enjoys catching mice out-rodents <u>inside</u> to be his guests.

OCTOBER 24 I spent watching the wolves as Kamots heard a mouse

the most enjoyable part of the day they moused in the dead grasses. and that began a tail-wagging

stalk. The rest of the pack keyed in on his interest and gathered around in a pouncing circle. They were all focused intently on the sound, inaudible to me, in the brush. Kamots lunged at the mouse when it tried to break away. In typical wolf behavior, he played with it and released it only to catch it again. And he did this until the mouse died of a coronary, I'm sure. It was clear this game had a distinct purpose – for the pups to watch and learn.

NOVEMBER 15 I fed a road kill to the pack today and Kamots was first to eat, which is typical for the alpha male in the pack. He approached the dead deer with an attitude of pure dominance – hackles, ears and tail raised. After asserting himself this way, he pulled the carcass back several yards before tearing away at it. Then, he allowed Matsi – who seems to be working himself into

Jim Dutcher

Jim Dutcher

Jim Dutcher

the second ranking, beta position – to share the kill with him. Matsi approached Kamots in the typical submissive style – crawling on his belly, tail down and wagging. Once Kamots gave him permission to eat the carcass, Matsi rose and defended the kill growling at perceived interlopers – Momoto, a magpie and a willow branch.

DECEMBER 30 After several weeks of relative quiet, the pack took up howling again today. I heard Kamots begin slowly and quietly build in volume and range. I never seem to be ready with my recording equipment during these perfect opportunities. Today, I decided to just let myself listen and feel, instead of worrying about recording levels and co-axial cables. The rest of the pack answered Kamots in chorus, each hitting a different note. With so much range, it sounded as though there were twenty wolves instead of the octet. I have always loved their howling but this time was incredible, maybe because I stood quietly in the meadow, letting the sound enter through my ears and exit through my heart.

JANUARY 9 I just skied in from town and hit a whiteout. The wind was a razor across the meadow, shaving off the tops of the drifts, throwing stinging snow into my eyes. If not for the willow markers I had placed every 20 feet along the trail, I'm sure I would still be out there. I knew I should have holed up when I got up this morning and my boots were frozen to the floor, even though I had stoked the stove four times during the night. The outhouse was particularly inhospitable because my fleece toilet seat cover had fallen in the night before. The view of the Sawtooths is spectacular but the 35 below temperature requires a short admiration time. The wolves who have enjoyed the cold weather until now seem surly, refusing to leave the shelter of the protective hollows they smoothed out in the snow.

97

Jim Dutcher

FEBRUARY 21   The pack is a matted, soggy, joyous mess. Temperatures climbed to 45 degrees, seeming balmy after so much cold. After a forever of frozen silence, there was suddenly the cacophony of thaw. Water dripped from branches and ran below the snow. I know it is only teasing spring but it feels like paradise. Matsi and Momoto took turns leading games of chase with their tails tucked, and ears pinned back. All the wolves joined in, running up and back, splashing in puddles and pinning each other in the slush. I may be projecting too many human qualities on these animals after spending more time with them than my own species. Anthropomorphic or not, I swear I saw crazy laughter on their faces.

MARCH 19   I woke up to the rattling call of sandhill cranes in the meadow. They have returned here to breed from their wintering grounds in Texas. Standing four feet tall they look impossibly exotic in this still winter-held landscape. Cranes evolved during a warm, humid Eocene, about 35 million years before the Rocky Mountains rose. Wolves have been padding around here for about two million years. For longer than I can fathom, the creatures that have inhabited this area have eaten each other, eluded each other and managed to co-exist. As we change so much of the earth's surface, we are forcing out many of her inhabitants, accelerating rates of extinction. At this point in time, in this beautiful place which harbors many threatened species, I wonder how we will all fit into the next epoch.

South of the Border Torta

*This meatless "pie" is made up of crisp corn tortillas layered with wonderfully
spicy fillings of fresh vegetables, beans, and cheeses. Serve with a spinach
salad and a pitcher of margaritas.*

3 cups cooked black or pinto beans (or a mixture of the two)
¹/₄ cup chicken stock
1 tablespoon vegetable oil
2 green bell peppers, cored, seeded, and julienned
2 zucchini, halved and thinly sliced
2 cups red onion, finely chopped
2 cloves garlic, minced
1 cup corn kernels (fresh works best)
1 teaspoon ground cumin
¹/₄ teaspoon cayenne pepper
salt and pepper to taste
6 (8-inch) blue corn tortillas
2 cups salsa
2 cups grated cheese (a mixture of mozzarella, provolone, and Monterey Jack)
chopped fresh cilantro for garnish

Preheat oven to 375°.

Puree the beans and chicken stock in a blender or food processor.
Set aside.

In a large skillet, heat the vegetable oil over medium heat. Add green bell
pepper, zucchini, red onion, and garlic. Sauté the vegetables for about 10
minutes, stirring often, until they are tender. Add the corn, cumin, cayenne,
and salt and pepper, and cook for another 3 minutes.

Oil an 8-inch springform pan with 3-inch sides. Place 1 tortilla on the
bottom of the pan, and spread ¹/₂ cup of the bean puree over the tortilla. Top
with 1 cup of the vegetable mixture, and then spoon ¹/₃ cup salsa over the
vegetables. Sprinkle ¹/₃ cup cheese over the salsa. Repeat this procedure until
you have used all of the ingredients, ending with cheese.

Bake for 45 minutes. Let sit for 5 minutes before removing from the pan.
Cut into wedges, and garnish with the cilantro.

Serves 10–12

Trader Jack's Artichoke and Shrimp

Jack McClosky, general manager of the Minnesota Timberwolves, is known throughout the N.B.A. as "Trader Jack." He's given us this rich recipe that makes a wonderful buffet dish or elegant supper.

6 ½ tablespoons butter, divided
4 ½ tablespoons flour
¾ cup milk
¾ cup heavy cream
salt and freshly ground pepper to taste
14-ounce can artichoke hearts, drained and quartered
1 pound shrimp, peeled, deveined, cooked, and chopped
1 pound fresh mushrooms, sliced
¼ cup dry sherry
1 tablespoon Worcestershire sauce
¼ cup grated Parmesan cheese
paprika

In a medium saucepan, melt 4½ tablespoons of butter over medium-low heat. Stir in the flour, and cook until bubbly, about 1–2 minutes. Gradually add milk and cream, stirring constantly with a whisk. When smooth, season with salt and pepper, and set aside.

Arrange artichoke hearts in a buttered 13x9x2-inch glass baking dish, or similar-sized round dish. Scatter shrimp over artichokes.

In a large skillet, melt remaining butter, add mushrooms, and sauté over high heat until brown. Spoon mushrooms over shrimp. Add sherry and Worcestershire sauce to cream sauce, and mix well. Pour over contents of baking dish. Sprinkle with Parmesan cheese and paprika. Bake for 30 minutes, or until bubbling. Serve at once.

Serves 6

Minnesota Timberwolves

When fans throughout Minnesota were summoned to find the perfect mascot for their new basketball team, they reached for the obvious with the Flies, the Mosquitoes, or the Jackrabbits. A down-to-earth populace not known for its flamboyant humor, Minnesotans also suggested such creative names as the Aquadrinks, the Double-dribblers, the Dullards, the Flakes, the Loon-A-Ticks, the Moosekateers, Shake and Bake, and the Yumpin Yaks. In the end, 842 city councils from around the state settled on the Timberwolves, an appropriate symbol since Minnesota is home to the largest population of timber wolves, or gray wolves, in the Lower 48 states.

Mister Rogers

In years to come, Fred Rogers' efforts to foster goodwill toward wolves may be one of the most effective educational tools ever used. A new generation of children raised on *Mr. Rogers' Neighborhood* is growing up with a different point of view—one where granny is not on the menu. Rogers presents common storybook tales like *Little Red Riding Hood* in a modern light. Rogers was ordained as a Presbyterian minister in 1962 with a charge to continue his work with children and families through the media. The life he leads off camera is directed and peaceful. At 6:30 every morning, Rogers swims laps. He is also a strict vegetarian and maintains his weight at a svelte 143. His favorite place on earth is The Crooked House, his rickety old home on Nantucket, Massachusetts.

Grandmother Rogers' Corn Pudding

This delicate sweet pudding is a family recipe that Grandmother Rogers made every Christmas. It takes five minutes to put together, and you'll probably need to make a double batch to keep up with the demand.

2 eggs
2 tablespoons all-purpose flour
17-ounce can cream-style corn
1/2 cup milk
2 tablespoons butter, melted
1/4 teaspoon salt

Preheat oven to 350°. Butter a 2-quart casserole. (A 9-inch square dish works well.)

Place eggs in a medium bowl, and beat well using a wire whisk. Sprinkle with flour, and whisk until smooth. Add all other ingredients and combine well. (Mixture will be runny.) Pour into prepared casserole, and bake for 1 hour.

Serves 6

New Skete Smoked Fowl Wild Rice Salad

Take this earthy salad to your next picnic. A good bottle of Chianti rounds out the meal.

> *3 whole smoked New Skete Farms chickens,*
> *or 1 whole smoked turkey breast,*
> *or 3 whole smoked ducks (or substitute local smoked fowl)*
> *1 cup shelled pecan halves*
> *1 tablespoon virgin olive oil*
> *1 ripe avocado*
> *juice of 1/2 lemon*
> *1 cup cooked long grain wild rice*
> *2 cups fresh black cherries, pitted*
> *1 tablespoon crisp bacon bits*
> *chopped scallions*
> *head of lettuce*
>
> *Vinaigrette:*
> *1/2 cup Grey Poupon mustard*
> *2 cloves garlic, finely minced*
> *3 twists from a pepper mill*
> *1/2 cup virgin olive oil*

If using chicken, remove skin and bones from the breasts. Tear or shred the breast meat into bite-sized pieces. If using turkey breast, slice thinly. If using duck, remove skin and bones, and slice meat thinly. (Roast the skin in a 350° oven for 10 minutes and use for garnish.)

Using a small skillet, sauté the pecans in the olive oil for several minutes. Set aside.

Peel and halve the avocado, remove the pit, and slice each half lengthwise into 6 slices. Place them on a plate, and coat with the lemon juice.

Place mustard, garlic, and pepper in a small bowl. Whisk quickly while slowly dribbling in oil. Set aside.

If using smoked chicken, mix it together with the wild rice in a large bowl. Toss in pecans, cherries, and vinaigrette (amount according to taste). Place a mound of this mixture on a bed of lettuce leaves in the center of a serving platter. If using smoked turkey or duck, place a mound of rice mixture on one side of the platter, and slices of the turkey or duck on the other side. Lay avocado slices in a fan shape over the rice. Sprinkle with the bacon bits and chopped scallions or chopped crispy duck skin. Serve slightly chilled.

Serves 6–8

Monks of New Skete

The Monks of New Skete belong to the Orthodox Church of America. Founded in 1966, the Monks have eleven members, who live a monastic life in Cambridge, New York. They are best known for training and breeding German Shepherd dogs and their two books, *How to Be Your Dog's Best Friend* and *The Art of Raising a Puppy*. They offer theses tips: To learn about your dog, learn about its ancestor, the wolf. To create an obedient pet and good friend, teach your puppy, that you, the owner, are the alpha by acting like an alpha. The Monks propose disciplining your dog as wolf elders discipline pups—hand it out sparingly, be firm but not harsh. Grabbing a young pup by the scruff of the neck and giving it a good shake communicates displeasure in a way a pup can understand.

Gladiola Montana

Gladiola Montana, author of *Never Ask a Man the Size of His Spread: A Cowgirl's Guide to Life,* shares some food for thought: If it takes you longer to figure out the recipe than it will to cook the dish, fix something else. A real cowgirl, Gladiola says she has been married twice and both her husbands are dead. She claims she did not kill them, but admits to having given it some thought. She did shoot one of them in the arm one time. It was an accident, she says, and he was a lot easier to get along with after that and they had a very happy marriage. Gladiola lives on a small ranch somewhere between Mexico and Canada with two dogs, a few horses, and some cattle.

Gladiola's Full House Steak

Here are a few of my observations on cooking: Any fool can eat, but it takes a cook to fix it. The best food is simple and not emotionally complicated. More meat goes bad in the oven than anywhere else. You can put your socks in the oven, but that don't make 'em biscuits. —G.M.

2 New York strip steaks, 8 to 10 ounces each

1 tablespoon canola oil
1 small yellow onion, minced
2 fresh hot chile peppers (serrano or poblano work well), cored, seeded, and minced
2 cloves garlic, pressed
1/2 cup grated Monterey Jack cheese
1 teaspoon coarse ground black pepper

Prepare coals for barbecuing.

Place the steaks on a cutting board, and slice a pocket into one side of each steak.

Heat the oil in a large skillet, and add the onion, chiles, and garlic. Sauté until transparent about 5–10 minutes. Remove from heat, place them in a small bowl, and mix in the cheese. The heat from the vegetables should soften the cheese a little.

Place pepper on a plate, and roll the sides of the steaks in it. They should be crusty with the pepper when you're through.

Fill the meat pockets with the vegetable-cheese mixture, and fasten closed with wooden toothpicks or skewers. Place steaks on the hot grill and cook according to your preference (3–4 minutes per side for medium-rare).

Serves 2

Souris à la Crème

In Never Cry Wolf, *based on his own experiences as a government biologist in Canada's barren Northwest Territories, Mowat sets out to prove that the white Arctic wolf is not responsible for appreciably threatening caribou populations. Watching and recording their habits, he discovers that the wolves gorge on mice in the warm months when the rodent's numbers explode. He guesses that the mice were plentiful enough to sustain a large carnivore and tests the theory on himself. Following is a French preparation that may or may not be as delectable as claimed. We tested but did not taste it.*

> *1 dozen fat mice*
> *1 cup white flour*
> *1 piece sowbelly (I should perhaps note that sowbelly is normally only available in the Arctic, but ordinary salt pork can be substituted)*
> *salt and pepper*
> *cloves*
> *ethyl alcohol*

Skin and gut the mice, but do not remove the heads; wash, then place in a pot with enough alcohol to cover the carcasses. Allow to marinate for about 2 hours. Cut sowbelly into small cubes and fry slowly until most of the fat has been rendered. Now remove the carcasses from the alcohol and roll them in a mixture of salt, pepper, and flour; then place in frying pan and sauté for about 5 minutes (being careful not to allow the pan to get too hot, or the delicate meat will dry out and become tough and stringy). Now add a cup of alcohol and 6 or 8 cloves. Cover the pan and allow to simmer slowly for 15 minutes. The cream sauce can be made according to any standard recipe. When the sauce is ready, drench the carcasses with it, cover, and allow to rest in a warm place for 10 minutes before serving.

Serves 1 starving back-country biologist

Farley Mowat

Ted Amsden

For more than three decades, Farley Mowat has written of the lands, animals, and people of the Far North in such classics as *The Dog Who Wouldn't Be*, *People of the Deer*, and *The Grey Seas Under*. Born in Belleville, Ontario, in 1921, Mowat has lived in Canada—as far north as possible—all of his life. The best-selling book, *Never Cry Wolf*, chronicles the Arctic summer Mowat spent studying wolves in the Canadian Keewatin Barrens, and became a plea for the conservation of wolves in the wild. The Soviet government banned the slaughter of wolves because of Mowat's entreaty. Mowat's *Sea of Slaughter* documents the devastating destruction of wildlife on the Eastern seaboard since the coming of the Europeans.

National Wildlife Federation

The Northern Rockies Natural Resource Center, located in Missoula, Montana, is one of nine field offices of the National Wildlife Federation. Much of its focus is on threatened and endangered species. The office's four employees work actively with state agencies and conservation groups to develop sound strategies for recovering wolves, grizzlies, and other rare species such as lynx and black-footed ferrets. Additionally, staff helped develop twenty-five hands-on wolf trunks that are loaned to school teachers in the region. The trunks contain wolf pelts, skulls, tracks, games, videos, books, and other activities to teach children about wild wolves.

Juan's Mexican Rice

When you're in a hurry, make the rice ahead of time for a quick side dish that goes well with Mexican food or barbecued chicken, pork, or beef. Add Linda Ronstadt's corn muffins for a complete meal.

¹/₄ pound bacon, cut into small pieces
1 small onion, finely chopped
1 celery stalk, chopped
8-ounce can tomato sauce
4-ounce can diced green chiles
1 tablespoon chili powder
2 cups cooked white rice
chopped fresh cilantro for garnish

Place bacon pieces in a medium skillet, and sauté until crisp. Remove bacon and set aside on a paper towel.

Add the onion and celery to the bacon drippings, and sauté until transparent, about 15 minutes. Drain off any excess fat. Add tomato sauce, green chiles, and chili powder, and combine well. Add the cooked rice and the bacon pieces, toss together, and heat through. Garnish with the fresh cilantro.

Serves 2–4

Chicken Creole

*A fail-safe dish that makes a tasty family meal when time is of the essence.
Serve with plenty of warm French bread.*

*1 medium onion, chopped
1 green bell pepper, cored, seeded, and chopped
1 tablespoon vegetable oil
2 cups diced cooked chicken
1 cup cooked white rice
2 cups Newman's Own spaghetti sauce
pinch of ground nutmeg*

In a large skillet, sauté onion and green pepper in oil until soft, 8–10 minutes. Stir in chicken, rice, spaghetti sauce, and nutmeg. Cover and simmer over low heat for 20 minutes, or bake at 350° for 20 minutes. Serve at once.

Serves 4

Paul Newman

Robert Norman

With Paul Newman there is no narcissistic life crisis or neurotic Hollywood behavior. The Oscar winner is committed to his family, his art, and a life of good works. Profits from the ubiquitous Newman's Own gourmet food products go to favorite charities. The Hole in the Wall Gang Camp, founded by Newman in 1988, treats children who have cancer or other life-threatening illnesses to a summer of boating, fishing, riding horses, swimming, theater, and pure fun. Located on 300 acres in the hills of northeastern Connecticut, the camp's buildings and furnishings have the ambiance of *Butch Cassidy and the Sundance Kid*. Newman lives with his wife of more than three decades, Joanne Woodward, in Westport, Connecticut, and New York.

Carter Niemeyer

Investigations by wildlife biologist Carter Niemeyer have proven that wolves are seldom responsible for the many livestock deaths they are often blamed for in Montana. Arriving at the scene of a slain animal, Niemeyer, an Animal Damage Control officer, can quickly decipher what kind of animal made the kill by examining the carcass. Ranchers respect Niemeyer for his honesty and easy-going manner. He is credited with turning around many ranchers' opinions about the wolf. Fellow wildlife biologists admire him for his intelligent insight into a changing future for Animal Damage Control, a federal agency frequently criticized by environmentalists.

Carter's Stew

My favorite recipe is stew because you can supplement the contents of the stew with various meats and vegetables, depending on your taste and preference. You can be creative and use any kind of meat—deer, elk, porcupine, possum, antelope, even beef. —C.N.

2 pounds stew meat, cut into 1-inch cubes
1 tablespoon olive oil
2–3 small onions, chopped
3 large carrots, peeled and sliced into rounds
2 medium potatoes, peeled and cut into 1/2-inch cubes
1 celery stalk, cut diagonally into 1-inch chunks
2–3 cups homemade or canned beef broth
14 1/2-ounce can tomatoes with liquid
2 tablespoons tapioca (optional)
2 teaspoons sugar
salt and pepper to taste
1/4 cup Burgundy wine (optional)

Preheat oven to 325°.

Heat oil in a Dutch oven. Add meat, and sauté over medium heat until browned on all sides, 7–10 minutes.

Add all other ingredients, cover, and bake for 3–4 hours, until the vegetables are tender. (Don't peek or disturb for the first 2 hours.) Ladle the stew into shallow soup bowls and serve with hot biscuits.

Serves 4–6

Dolly Parton's Apple Stack Cake

When on tour, Dolly, her band, and road crew enjoy roadside picnics with homemade foods rather than stopping at restaurants.

Dolly Parton

Sam Emerson

Cakes:	Filling:
4 eggs, lightly beaten	2 pounds apples
1 cup sugar	(Granny Smith or Gravenstein),
2/3 cup milk	peeled, cored, and thinly sliced
1/2 cup molasses	1 cup water
1 teaspoon cinnamon	1 cup sugar
1 teaspoon vanilla extract	1/2 teaspoon ground cinnamon
6 cups self-rising cake flour	1/4 teaspoon ground allspice
1/2 teaspoon baking soda	
1 cup (2 sticks) butter, softened	

Preheat oven to 300°. Butter and flour six 9-inch round cake pans.

To prepare the cakes: In a large mixing bowl, beat together eggs, sugar, milk, molasses, cinnamon, and vanilla until smooth.

Sift together flour and baking soda. Add butter, and blend with fingertips until it resembles bread crumbs. Add this to the egg mixture, and combine until it looks like bread dough.

Turn onto a floured surface, and knead for about 1 minute. Divide the dough into 6 equal balls, and roll out each ball into a thin 8-inch round. Place each layer of dough into a separate cake pan, and press flat. Bake for 15–20 minutes. Remove from oven, and let cakes cool in pans.

To prepare filling: Place apple slices and water in a medium saucepan, and cook over medium heat until soft, about 15 minutes. Strain, and discard water. Add sugar, cinnamon, and allspice, and cook over low heat until sugar is dissolved and mixture is thick. Set aside to cool.

To assemble: Place filling between cake layers and stack 1 layer on top of the other. Repeat this procedure using all layers of cake and all of the filling. This recipe will make two 3-layer cakes, or one 6-layer cake, and is best when refrigerated for 2–3 days.

Serves 10–12

Everyone loves Dolly. There's a lot to love in that five-foot frame and 40-20-36 figure. Born into poverty and a family of twelve in Sevier County, Tennessee, Dolly knew at a tender age that she would be the first member of her family in generations to leave the mountains and go out into the world. She began writing songs and singing at seven years old and by ten she had made her professional debut. Today, Dolly is known for her bawdy talk, trampy look, many talents, $100 million-plus fortune, and huge heart. Still, Dolly has not forgotten her humble Smoky Mountain roots. She established the Dollywood Foundation, a nonprofit organization benefiting children in her home community through scholarships, teacher training, computer labs, graduation incentives, and other programs.

Doug Arapaho Peacock

Doug Tompkins

Feeling war-weary after returning from two tours as a Green Beret medic in Vietnam, Doug Peacock retreated to the wilderness. The book *Grizzly Years: In Search of the American Wilderness* is his account of two decades spent in the rugged mountains of Montana and Wyoming, alone and unarmed among the grizzly bears.

During those years, wilderness became more than an idea; for him, it became home, the original landscape. Peacock appears like the grizzly bear he has devoted his life to saving. A big man with a dark, profuse beard, he is shy, self-contained, and aggressive only when provoked. When not in the backcountry with grizzlies, he lives with his wife, Lisa, outside Tucson, Arizona.

Aztec Wild Turkey Lobo Style

1 Aztec wild turkey (I can't tell you where; consult your conscience)

Tarahumara stuffing: (sauté for 4 minutes)
chopped giblets
¹/₂ cup diced onion
1 head garlic, sliced
2 cups diced matsutake mushrooms (Armillaria ponderosa: found with Mexican wild turkeys and lobos, under live oak, Texas madrone, and manzanita thickets above 8,000 feet in the eastern outliers of the Sierra Madre)
combine with:
4 cups shredded stale Tarahumara corn tortillas
¹/₂ cup pine nuts (use whitebark pine in northern wolf range)
¹/₄ cup fresh wild green chilepiquin peppers, chopped
1–2 tablespoons fresh wild sage (use younger leaves, taste first as strength of wild sage varies tremendously)
1 tablespoon fresh wild oregano
1 cup mixed fruit (use dried Saguaro cactus fruit or substitute half diced crabapple and half either dried elderberries or wild grapes parboiled for 5 minutes)
salt, pepper, fresh thyme, and basil to taste (salt lightly)
1 dozen Mearns' quail eggs, beat in to moisten

Baste: (melt and simmer for ¹/₂ hour)
1 cup javelina oil (rendered fat of javelina sweetened with 1 teaspoon of wild honey, or use half olive oil and half butter)
1 cup fresh cilantro, finely diced
10 limes, juiced

Glaze:
¹/₂ cup manzanita jelly
¹/₂ cup organ pipe cactus jam
2 cups Bacanora mescal (distilled "tequila" from wild agaves)
3 tablespoons fresh wild red chilepiquin peppers, chopped
¹/₂ cup fresh lime juice
2 tablespoons suitable oil or butter, melted

Preheat oven to 500°.

Pluck turkey gently and pat dry. Allow bird to achieve room temperature.

Stuff turkey cavity and crop with Tarahumara stuffing but allow for expansion. Suture up with 3/0 silk. Baste or coat all surfaces with the basting mixture. Place, uncovered, in hot oven. Turn oven down to 400° and bake without opening oven for first 30 minutes. Baste efficiently at 20–30 minute intervals, not allowing heat to escape.

After first 2 hours, cover breast with cloth soaked in drippings (the precise timetable will vary according to size and age of bird; this one of 4 hours is for a young tom about 12 pounds. Don't dry it out; if necessary, resort to braising and moist cooking).

During last hour, turn down heat to 300°, remove cloth gingerly from breast. Mix glaze ingredients in a small bowl. Baste with glaze several times during the last 30 minutes. Pour what's left of the glaze over the bird just before you remove it from the oven. Have a shot of mescal, and let the turkey rest for 20 minutes.

Serves 12–14

This recipe is for the dinner I intended to cook for wolf-people Tom Rush and Renee Askins to repay their hospitality for putting me up in the valley below the Tetons—a many-splendored night, as they say. Actually, there were several, though I am thinking of one in particular.

The reason I failed to deliver is because these wild birds are hard to come by. Though they once ranged into southern Arizona, today the closest Aztec, the white-tipped or Gould's race of wild turkey, live in Chihuahua, where wild Mexican wolves, jaguars, and a last grizzly still roam. On my way down to bag the turkey, my pickup broke down.

It was just past Casas Grande when I felt a high-speed shimmy in the drive-train, then the whine and rumble of something about to pop on the rear drive-shaft. I didn't dare just pull over, leave the truck, and go for a part, since it would take a day or two, and the odds of returning to a burned-out, engine-less, hull of steel propped up on blocks with all four wheels gone would be excellent.

So I pushed on south towards my Aztec Turkey range. Twenty minutes later, I heard that nauseating scream of the needle bearings in the front universal joint splintering and freezing, the drive-shaft breaking off, dropping from its front anchor. The heavy shaft was now hanging under the pickup like a giant metallic phallus and scraping along the potted pavement. When it finally lodged in a pothole, catapulting the truck at fifty miles per hour through the air, I knew my wild turkey trip was all over.

Sorry, I got sidetracked. Back to the recipe. The idea behind this dish is to cook something—using wild food—a wolf would love, especially a lobo or white Mexican wolf. The key, of course, is a Mexican wild turkey, though other wild races of Meleagris gallapavo *will substitute admirably. This glaze/stuffing combo will also work with a storebought turkey, though the flavor is much inferior to that of a wild bird. Incidentally, our domestic turkey was derived from the Mexican Aztec turkey: when the Aztecs took over the Valley of Mexico they brought their semi-domesticated turkeys with them from the north. The Spaniards shipped these birds to Spain. The Aztec turkey was domesticated in Europe and returned to northeastern North America as our barnyard variety. Three hundred years of agricultural tinkering has transformed these beautiful creatures into beasts that can't effect a cloacal kiss (mate) because they have been bred for absurdly large breasts and has turned one of the most intelligent animals in the wild into dim-witted birds so stupid they drown in the rain cuz they forget to close their mouths.*

Don't mess with wild nature, especially when cooking! —D.A.P.

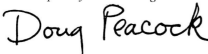

The Mystery Woman's Mango Chutney

© Ann Mullowney

Ridley Pearson

What makes Ridley Pearson, a grown man, strap himself into a harness and climb trees? To feel the exuberance of youth, and to escape the pressures of producing best-selling forensic thrillers. But Pearson doesn't have much time for the new sport. He has written ten books in ten years, including *Undercurrents*, *The Angel Maker*, *No Witnesses*, and *Chain of Evidence*. In addition, he collaborated with Stephen King, Dave Barry, and Amy Tan, among others, on *MidLife Confidential: The Rock Bottom Remainders Tour America with Three Chords and an Attitude*. A self-professed workaholic, he takes his work with him everywhere. He once used solar panels to power his computer on a beach in Mexico; he frequently holes up to write in his yurt in Idaho.

In days of old (if you ask me) lemon was offered with fish because the fish itself had not seen the great waters in far too long, and bacteria clung to it like barnacles to the boat bottom. The lemon "freshened" the flavor, actually chemically cooking the bacteria, and removing, or at least masking, that "fishy" smell. These days, even in the Wood River Valley, we see incredibly fresh fish— maybe not sushi quality, but damn close. The result is that grilled, poached, baked, and broiled fish can pretty much stand alone—a little tamari and a sprig of basil and you're set. But for those who want to dress up a fish dish without increasing the chance of heart failure or requiring an extra thirty minutes at the athletic club, I offer a recipe first fed to me by a mysterious woman of unparalleled beauty, elegance, and fine taste. This mystery woman referred to the dish as a "salsa," but it seemed to me more of a "chutney," and the two of us, rightly or wrongly, decided that a salsa differed from a chutney in that a chutney is cooked, while a salsa is prepared raw. Someone will no doubt set us straight on this qualification. The Mystery Woman's Chutney is simple, fast, and consistently receives rave reviews, something every author envies. —R.P.

2 mangoes, peeled and chopped
$^1/_4$–$^3/_4$ cup sugar (to taste)
$^1/_4$ cup finely chopped red pepper
2 tablespoons grated fresh ginger
2 tablespoons white vinegar
$^1/_2$ teaspoon ground cloves
$^1/_2$ teaspoon turmeric
juice of 3 limes
$^1/_4$ cup chopped fresh cilantro

Combine all ingredients, except cilantro, in a medium saucepan. Bring to a boil over medium heat, stirring constantly. Lower heat, and simmer for 10 minutes. Remove from heat and let cool.

Stir in cilantro. Spoon generously over fish of choice.

Serves 6–8

Ridley Pearson

North Carolina Oxtail Soup

This soup is best when served hot with homemade biscuits, and provides many meals to a large "pack." The prepared soup readily freezes and does not lose any flavor once thawed and reheated. —M.P.

1 tablespoon olive oil
6–8 pieces of oxtail
1 large onion, cut into bite-sized pieces
1 teaspoon salt
1–2 teaspoons black pepper to taste
1/2 head green cabbage, shredded
6 large carrots, peeled and cut into 1/2-inch slices
4 large baking potatoes, peeled and cut into 1-inch cubes
2 cans (16 ounces each) whole, peeled, or chopped tomatoes

Heat olive oil in a large soup pot. Add the oxtails, and brown them well in several batches over medium-high heat, setting each batch aside until all are browned.

Place the chopped onion in the pot, and sauté until brown, stirring frequently so it does not burn. Return all oxtails to the pot, and add enough water to just cover the oxtails and onion. Add the salt and pepper, and bring to a boil over medium heat. Reduce heat, cover and simmer for about 2 hours.

Remove oxtails, and set aside to cool. Add cabbage, carrots, and potatoes to the pot. Pour in the tomato juice from the cans, then quarter the tomatoes and add them to the pot. (Add the whole cans at once if using chopped tomatoes.)

Remove all of the meat from the oxtails, and place it back into the pot. Add water so that the pot is three-fourths full. Simmer over medium-low heat for 1–2 hours. Adjust seasonings if necessary, and ladle into soup bowls.

Serves 8–10

Mike Phillips

When Europeans first colonized America, the red wolf ranged over the entire East Coast. But by 1980 after years of human persecution, the red wolf was declared extinct in the wild. Seven years later, the U.S. Fish and Wildlife Service released captive-born wolves into northeastern North Carolina in the first-ever attempt to restore a species that no longer existed outside of zoos. The program has proven to be a success, and today, more than sixty-five of these cinnamon- and tawny-colored wolves run free. Mike Phillips, who was the Red Wolf Recovery Program field coordinator, says the program demonstrates that restoring an endangered species should always be considered an alternative to extinction and that humans and wolves can coexist. Phillips presently heads wolf recovery efforts in Yellowstone National Park.

Brad Pitt

At heart, Brad Pitt is a laid-back country boy. Pitt says Los Angeles is his base, but for this Southern native, the Ozarks will always be home. With his film earnings, Pitt bought a tract of woods on home ground where his dogs Deacon, Earl, and Maggie can run free. However, Pitt is too busy to take time away from filming to spend much time there. Until then, the dogs are mostly confined to Pitt's Jeep Cherokee, which he admits is a pit. After the triumphant *Thelma & Louise* and *A River Runs Through It*, Pitt has chosen interesting, difficult projects such as *Interview with a Vampire*, *Legends of the Fall*, *Seven*, and *12 Monkeys*.

My Mom's Breakfast Casserole

Brad Pitt loves his mother's cooking and has provided us with a favorite recipe. Its aroma is sure to lure everyone from the sleepy warmth of their beds.

1 pound mild sausage
6 eggs
2 cups milk
1 teaspoon dried mustard
1 teaspoon salt
2 cups cubed bread crusts
8 ounces shredded Cheddar cheese

Brown sausage in a medium skillet. Drain and discard any fat, and set aside to cool.

Lightly beat the eggs in a large mixing bowl. Add milk, mustard powder, and salt, and blend well. Stir in bread crusts, sausage, and cheese, and mix well. Pour into a shallow 2-quart glass baking dish, and refrigerate overnight.

Preheat oven to 350°. Bake for 40–45 minutes, or until edges are brown. Cut into wedges and serve hot or at room temperature.

Serves 6–8

Toscana's Tagliatelle Ragù

This tantalizing pasta dish is Paula's favorite when dining at Toscana Restaurant in Brentwood, California. It is submitted on her behalf by executive chef Agostino Sciandri. Freshly grated Parmesan cheese and warmed garlicky French bread completes the picture.

2 celery stalks
1 medium carrot
1 medium yellow onion
2 cloves garlic
4 tablespoons olive oil
8 ounces lean ground beef
2 cups red wine (Cabernet or Chianti)
16-ounce can peeled whole tomatoes
2 bay leaves
salt and pepper to taste
freshly grated Parmesan cheese
1 pound tagliatelle pasta

Using a food processor, finely chop celery, carrot, onion, and garlic.

Heat the olive oil in a medium skillet, and add the vegetables and ground beef. Cook, uncovered, over medium heat for 25 minutes. Add the red wine and allow to evaporate, about 10 minutes.

Finely chop the tomatoes (including their juice) in the food processor. Add them to the sauce along with the bay leaves, and stir to combine. Simmer gently, uncovered, for 1 hour, stirring occasionally. Remove bay leaves, and season with salt and pepper.

Prepare pasta according to package directions. Drain, and divide equally among 4 heated plates. Ladle sauce over pasta, sprinkle with Parmesan cheese, and serve immediately.

Serves 4

Paula Poundstone

Humorist Paula Poundstone says she is not exactly an environmental hero. "I drive a car, I eat meat, I've bitten children, I wear leather, sometimes I've been very tired and used a paper towel." But Poundstone recycles faithfully, buys products made from recycled materials, and avoids disposable items when she can. She says people don't realize there's a middle ground between bathing in cold water for the rest of your life and in making simple conservation efforts. Poundstone, who has twice won the CableACE award for comedy, is a talented writer as well, and is a contributing editor for *Mother Jones* magazine. She lives in L.A. with her foster daughter and six cats.

Wolf It Down Meat Loaf

I go a little heavy on the garlic and the jalapeños because people in Arizona love hot garlicky dishes. If you don't, use them in lesser amounts.   B.H.

2 pounds lean ground beef
1 green bell pepper, diced
1 small yellow onion, diced
2 jalapeño peppers, fresh or canned, diced
2 cloves garlic, finely minced
2 eggs, lightly beaten
1 cup rolled oats
1 teaspoon baking powder
16-ounce can stewed tomatoes, diced
1/2 cup tomato ketchup
1/2 teaspoon salt
1/4 teaspoon black pepper

Preheat oven to 375°. Lightly grease two 9x5x3-inch loaf pans, or a 13x9-inch baking dish.

Using a large mixing bowl, combine all ingredients in the order listed. For easiest mixing—dive in and use your hands. Be sure to thoroughly combine all ingredients. Spread in prepared pans. Bake for 45–50 minutes, or until edges start to pull away from pan. (A fork inserted in the middle will reveal browned meat.)

Remove meat loaf from the oven, and let it rest in the pan for 5 minutes. Remove it from the pan, cover it loosely with aluminum foil, and let it rest an additional 5–10 minutes before slicing.

Serves 8–10

Grilled Utah Trout on R.R. Ranch Greens with Yogurt Lemon Dressing

Robert Redford

Sundance chef Don Heidel contributes this recipe from the Tree Room for Robert Redford. Fresh organic greens, grown on the premises, and locally made yogurt make this entrée a favorite.

Dressing:
1 lemon
1/2 cup lowfat yogurt
1 teaspoon chopped fresh thyme
1 teaspoon clover honey

4 boned fresh trout fillets (8–10 ounces each)
2 tablespoons olive oil
1 tablespoon cracked black pepper
1 pound baby greens, washed
2 tablespoons pine nuts, toasted

Prepare coals for grilling.

Remove 1 teaspoon zest from lemon, and juice the lemon. In a small bowl, blend the zest and juice with the yogurt, thyme, and honey. Refrigerate for 1–2 hours.

Brush trout with olive oil, and sprinkle with pepper. Place on oiled grill, flesh side down, for 8–10 minutes, depending on size of fillets. (Fish should flake easily when tested with a fork.)

Cover 4 plates with baby greens, and place 1 trout on top. Pour a small amount of dressing over, and garnish with pine nuts. Chef Heidel suggests finishing the plates with chive blossoms.

Serves 4

In 1961 before Robert Redford was a famous director and actor, he bought two acres in Utah's Provo Canyon, where he designed and built a home for his family. Today, Sundance sprawls over 5,000 acres and has become a mecca for environmentalists, alternative film makers, and those seeking an alternative to the crowded, high-gloss resort scene. The rustic retreat reflects Redford's commitment to the environment and his refined taste. Handhewn cedar lodges seem to grow from the land. Navajo rugs and classic western antiques fill the interiors and the retreat's kitchens serve organic herbs and vegetables grown on the Sundance Farm. Redford advances wolf recovery as an advisory board member to The Wolf Fund and in public presentations.

Linda Ronstadt

Robert Blakeman

The culture and beat of the Southwest has impassioned Linda Ronstadt. As a child growing up in Tucson, Arizona, Ronstadt listened to her father's assortment of Mexican ranchero recordings, her older sister's Hank Williams collection, the top 40, and gospel music broadcast by KFRF, a Mexican radio station just across the border. These elements have swayed Ronstadt's music, which embodies not only fire and heartache, but womanly wit as well. She made her debut in 1967 with the group Stone Poneys and followed with twenty-seven other albums, including seven Grammy awards and sales of over thirty million records.

Corn Muffins

Corn and cornmeal have been staples in the Southwestern kitchen for generations. Linda combines these traditional ingredients in this updated recipe for a healthy muffin that doesn't sacrifice taste.

1 cup whole wheat flour
1 cup coarsely ground yellow cornmeal
$^1/_4$ cup sugar
4 teaspoons baking powder
$^1/_2$ teaspoon salt (optional)
2 eggs, lightly beaten
1 cup skim milk
8$^1/_2$-ounce can (1 cup) cream-style corn
3 tablespoons butter, melted

Preheat oven to 425°. Generously butter 12 muffin cups.

In a large bowl, stir together the flour, cornmeal, sugar, baking powder, and salt.

In a medium bowl, combine the eggs, milk, corn, and butter. Add this to the dry ingredients, stirring until well combined.

Spoon the batter into the prepared muffin cups, and bake for 20–25 minutes, or until the tops are golden.

Makes 12 muffins

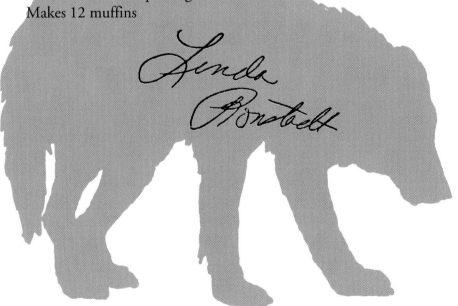

Red Velvet Cake

*The buttermilk in this perfect birthday cake gives the
chocolate a tang. Kids love it.*

1/2 cup vegetable shortening, softened
1 1/2 cups sugar
2 eggs
2 tablespoons cocoa powder
2 ounces red food coloring
2 1/4 cups all-purpose flour
1 teaspoon salt
1 cup buttermilk
1 teaspoon vanilla extract
1 tablespoon white vinegar
1 teaspoon baking soda

Cream cheese frosting:
4 ounces cream cheese, softened
1 1/2 cups confectioners' sugar
1 teaspoon vanilla extract

Preheat oven to 350°. Butter and flour two 9-inch round cake pans.

To prepare cake: Using an electric mixer, cream shortening and sugar
together in a large bowl. Add eggs and beat well. In a small bowl or cup,
make a paste of the cocoa and food coloring, and add to the
creamed mixture.

Sift together flour and salt twice. Add alternating with the buttermilk to
the creamed mixture. Stir in the vanilla.

Put the vinegar in a deep glass or bowl, and add the baking soda (it will
foam). When blended, stir it into the creamed cake batter. Do not beat, just
blend well with a wooden spoon.

Pour batter into prepared cake pans. Bake until the cake has pulled away
from the sides of the pans, and a knife inserted in the center comes out clean,
25–30 minutes. Let the cakes cool in the pans for 10 minutes, then turn
them out onto wire racks. Let them completely cool before frosting.

To prepare frosting: Cream all ingredients together with an electric mixer
until fluffy and smooth. Spread a thin layer of frosting over 1 cake layer.
Place the second layer on top, and spread the remaining frosting over the top
and sides of the cake.

Serves 8–10

Willard Scott

Willard Scott once described himself
as "the last great cornball in
America." Both his fans and his
critics agree, although his fans greatly
outnumber his detractors, since Scott
is often credited with the *Today*
show's top ratings. Scott's act is no
act; he is innately cheerful and kind.
In 1988, he was honored by the Casa
De Los Niños, a home for needy
children in Tucson, Arizona, for
helping its founder Sister Mary
Kathleen raise the money needed to
build a new wing. Scott and his wife,
Mary, own a farm in Virginia, where
they grow fruits and vegetables and
make homemade wine from their own
grapes. They also have a home in Big
Sky, Montana, just north of
Yellowstone National Park.

Maria Shriver and Arnold Schwarzenegger

Zade Rosenthal

If Maria Shriver and Arnold Schwarzenegger were wolves, they would be considered the definitive "alpha pair." They are ahead of the pack. He is one of the highest paid movie stars of all time, earning at least $15 million per film. She has made a name for herself on *Dateline NBC* as one of the nation's most respected television journalists. They live part time in Sun Valley, where Arnold carpools his pack of three around town in his quasi-military vehicle, the Hummer. The kids love the ride. Maria, well... she has disliked it from the beginning.

Maria's Oriental Chicken Salad

This fabulous salad was created by Micheal Rosen, a chef at Schatzi, a Schwarzenegger-Shriver venture in Santa Monica, California.

Marinade for chicken:
1 cup low-sodium soy sauce
3 ounces green onions, chopped
$1^1/_2$ ounces ginger, peeled and julienned
2–3 ounces dark sesame oil
salt and pepper to taste
2 pounds boneless chicken breasts

$^1/_4$–$^1/_2$ pound mixed lettuce greens
1 head iceberg lettuce
1 bunch watercress, tops only
1 bunch cilantro
1 bunch mint, leaves only
1 large carrot
1 small cucumber
3 large oranges

Sesame rice wine vinaigrette:
1 cup rice wine vinegar
$^1/_2$ cup peanut oil
$^1/_4$ cup sugar or to taste
2 tablespoons dark sesame oil
1 tablespoon low-sodium soy sauces
salt and coarsely ground black pepper to taste
$^1/_2$ teaspoon crushed red chile pepper

$^1/_2$ cup toasted slivered almonds
1 pinch pickled ginger
fried wonton skins for garnish

To prepare chicken: Combine all marinade ingredients in a baking dish. Add salt and black pepper to taste. Place chicken breasts in the dish, and refrigerate, preferably overnight. Preheat oven to 350°. Pour off and discard marinade. Bake chicken, skin side up, for 30 minutes, or until cooked through. Cool, and remove skin. Shred chicken.

To prepare salad: Clean lettuces, spin dry, and chill for crispness. Mix watercress, mint, and cilantro with lettuces. Peel and julienne the carrot and cucumber. Peel and segment the oranges.

To prepare vinaigrette: Whisk all vinaigrette ingredients together in a bowl.

To assemble salad: Place all ingredients except wonton skins in a large mixing bowl. Dress lightly with vinaigrette and toss gently. Add more dressing as required. Garnish with crumbled wonton skins.

Serves 4

Helen's Walnut Wolf Cake

Tom enjoys messing around in the kitchen, especially baking. He buys the finest Northwest walnuts at Seattle's Pike Street Market.

1 cup all-purpose flour
1 cup sugar
1 teaspoon baking powder
1/2 tablespoon salt
1 tablespoon cinnamon
1/2 cup butter, melted
1/2 cup milk
2 eggs, separated
2/3 cup coarsely chopped walnuts

Preheat oven to 350°. Butter and flour a 9-inch round cake pan (a rectangular pan works fine also).

Sift together flour, sugar, baking powder, salt, and cinnamon in a medium bowl.

In a separate bowl, whisk together the melted butter, milk, and egg yolks. Add this mixture to the flour mixture, and stir to combine.

Place the egg whites in a clean bowl, and using an electric mixer, beat on high speed until stiff peaks form, about 2 minutes. Fold egg whites and walnuts into the cake batter, and pour into prepared pan. Bake for 40 minutes, or until a toothpick inserted in the middle comes out clean. Cool, bite, howl.

Serves 8

Tom Skerritt

Tom Skerritt divides his time between Seattle and the San Juan Islands because he likes the easy-going people and the dramatic blues of the coastal weather. In an effort to spend more time in the Pacific Northwest, Skerritt has developed a Seattle-based independent film production company, ShadowCatcher Entertainment, named for the Native American word for photographer. In his spare time, the Emmy-winning star of CBS's *Picket Fences* is a wood carver, painter, and writer. He is also involved in community work and is especially committed to two favorite causes— protection of the environment and support for the homeless.

the hunt

the wolf has evolved over the millennia to be an excellent hunter. Its nose is exceedingly sensitive and can smell prey up to 1 mile away if the wind is right; that is 100 times more powerful than the human nose. Once on the trail of prey, the wolf may run at an all-day pace of 5 or 6 miles per hour. Wolves' peripheral vision is exceptionally keen. Because of this refined vision, a wolf notices movement far away. Wolves can hear high-pitched noises, sometimes from up to 6 miles away, making their auditory capability their keenest sense. Some biologists believe that wolves hunt more by sound than by smell.

Still, given all of these evolutionary advantages, hunting large hoofed animals such as moose, elk, caribou, and deer is an even contest for the wolf. The wolf's prey, too, have evolved with their own survival traits. Caribou and other game run at speeds much faster than the wolf. The wolf sprints at 35 miles an hour, a caribou 40. Moose often escape by swimming away from the slower dog-paddling wolf. A deer's sharp hooves and lightning reflexes might add up to a broken leg or shoulder, leading to starvation for a wolf. Because of the hoofed animals' superior agility and speed, the wolf evolved as a pack animal, relying on numbers and strategy to trap and kill its prey.

Wolves are shrewd. They sometimes watch a herd for days, stalking the weak, sick, and old. When a wolf comes within sight of its prey, often the predator and prey lock in eye contact. Author Barry Lopez calls this the "conversation of death." Biologists have recorded that when a moose or a deer stares back at a wolf and refuses to run, the wolf typically backs down. However, if the prey runs, the wolf chases. The chase may go on for days, or the kill may be over in less than a minute.

For every deer killed, about nine get away. But when an animal is downed, a wolf is quick to finish it. Its 42 teeth are designed to seize, tear, and crush. Its jaw has the power—1,500 pounds per square inch—to crush the large bones of his prey, even the large femur of an elk or moose.

I called this exchange in which the animals appear to lock eyes and make a decision the conversation of death. It is a ceremonial exchange, the flesh of the hunted in exchange for respect for its spirit. In this way both animals, not the predator alone, choose for the encounter to end in death. There is, at least, a sacred order in this. There is nobility. And it is something that happens only between the wolf and his major prey species. It produces, for the wolf, sacred meat.

—Barry Lopez, *Of Wolves and Men*

Jim Brandenburg

I've seen a pack try to awaken its sleeping leader. The pack members are obviously anxious to hunt, but they do not set out until the leader is ready, and the hunt is usually prefaced by a rousing chorus of howls. There is an air of excitement as the wolves get ready, a building of camaraderie, a joyousness. It isn't so very different than the behavior of your own dog when you announce that you're taking her out for a walk or some other excursion: You see a raised level of intensity, a fear of being left behind, happy relief at being underway , and a seriousness about the excursion.

—Jim Brandenburg, *Brother Wolf*

Jim Brandenburg

Firth Pocket Bread with Beef Filling

You'll get raves from the cowhands when you serve this portable Gucci-food out on the range.

Dough:
1 package (2 teaspoons) active dry yeast
1¹/₃ cups warm water (105°-115°)
1 teaspoon salt
¹/₄ teaspoon sugar
1 tablespoon olive oil
3–3¹/₂ cups all-purpose flour
cornmeal

Meat filling:
2 tablespoons cooking oil (corn, olive, or safflower)
1¹/₂ cups finely chopped onion
¹/₂ cup pine nuts
2 pounds lean ground beef
2 tomatoes, peeled and chopped
¹/₂ cup chopped green pepper
¹/₃ cup chopped fresh parsley
¹/₃ cup freshly squeezed lemon juice
3 tablespoons red wine vinegar
1¹/₂ teaspoons salt
³/₄ teaspoon allspice
¹/₂ teaspoon cayenne pepper

To prepare pocket bread: Dissolve yeast in warm water in a large mixing bowl. Add salt, sugar, oil, and half the flour. Stir until smooth. Add enough of the remaining flour to make the dough easy to handle. Turn dough onto a lightly floured surface, and knead until smooth and elastic, about 10 minutes. Shape dough into a ball. Place in greased bowl, cover, and let rise in a warm place until doubled, about 1 hour. Punch it down and divide dough into 6 equal balls. Let these rise for 30 minutes, covered, on a greased tray.

To prepare meat filling: While dough is rising, heat oil in a large skillet over medium heat. Add onion and pine nuts, and sauté, stirring often, until pine nuts are brown and onion is tender. Add ground beef, and brown, stirring constantly to break up the pieces. Pour off fat, add all remaining ingredients, and combine well. Reduce heat to low and simmer, uncovered, until all liquid is absorbed. Keep warm.

Preheat oven to 500°. Sprinkle 3 baking sheets with cornmeal. Roll each ball of dough into a round ¹/₈ inch thick. Place 2 rounds in opposite corners of each baking sheet, and let rise for 30 minutes more. Bake until loaves are puffed and light brown, about 10 minutes. Cut in half crosswise, and fill each half with prepared meat filling. Serve immediately, or place warm unfilled bread in plastic bags to keep moist and pliable until ready to serve.

Serves 6

Sleepy Valley Ranch

It is Idaho rancher Charlotte Reid's wish that someday she and her grandchildren will be able to hear the wolf's howl from her porch swing. Reid says that a rural upbringing and her father's teachings shaped her desire to live with nature rather than dominate it. As a youngster, Reid lived on a ranch that was so remote the directions called for visitors to drive 120 miles from the nearest town and turn east after the second antelope herd. Now she lives on the Sleepy Valley Ranch in Firth, where necessary predators like the coyote and prairie rattler have free range. She is a former advisory board member of the Wolf Education and Research Center.

Donald Snow

Donald Snow is the founder and associate editor of *Northern Lights* magazine in Missoula, Montana. The magazine brings together new voices from the American West—Terry Tempest Williams, Gretel Ehrlich, Jim Harrison, Edward Abbey, and others— through their essays, short stories, and poems. The quarterly magazine explores the cultural, political, and economic fabric of the region. An environmental activist, Snow was born in the mining camp of Hiawatha, Utah. He has authored two books, *Inside the Environmental Movement* and *Voices from the Environmental Movement*.

Howling Leg of Lamb

I choose lamb because of its place in Christian iconography, because my Mormon grandfather raised sheep until his allergies to sheep dip nearly killed him, and of course because of the wolf's obvious fondness for it. You just don't hear about wolves killing for tofu. Let's keep the world as unsafe as possible. The hardest part of this dish is getting the lamb leg ready to stuff. If you're a confident meat cutter (I am not), remove the bone from the lamb leg and flay it open. For instructions and helpful diagrams, you can use Joy of Cooking *or early Army training manuals. Otherwise, ask a good butcher to bone and butterfly it. If you want good sex, don't ever, ever, serve lamb with mint jelly. Mint jelly with lamb is one of the unqualified evils of the British empire. —D.S.*

leg of lamb (5–6 pounds), boned and butterflied

1 large red or yellow bell pepper
1 dozen whole cloves garlic
1 cup very good olive oil
6 ounces cracked green olives, pitted
2–4 ounces sun-dried tomatoes, packed in olive oil

3 fresh chipotle peppers, cored, seeded, and minced
2 1/2 cups dry white wine
3 bay leaves, crumbled
1 small red onion, sliced
the rest of the bottle of that same white wine

Broil bell pepper, turning it until the skin blackens and blisters on all sides. Peel, core, and seed it. (Be careful with the hot juice inside—it'll burn the hell out of you.) Slice into strips.

Sauté the garlic in the olive oil until slightly golden. Remove garlic, and reserve the scented oil. Chop the olives and tomatoes coarsely, then toss together with the garlic cloves, roasted pepper, chipotles, and a few splashes of the reserved olive oil.

Stuff butterflied leg with the olive mixture. Sprinkle it lightly with sea salt and coarse black pepper. Roll it up and tie with kitchen twine.

In a deep-sided bowl, whisk together the reserved olive oil and 2 1/2 cups of wine. Add the bay leaves and onion. Marinate the lamb in this mixture overnight in the refrigerator, or 3–4 hours at room temperature.

Preheat oven to 425°. Place the meat on a roasting rack in a baking pan. Roast 15 minutes on one side, then 15 minutes on the other. Drop temperature to 350°, and roast for about 75 minutes more for medium-rare. Skim the fat from the pan, and deglaze remaining juices on top of the stove with about 3/4 cup of wine. Reduce, adjust seasonings, and spoon sauce over the sliced lamb on a serving platter.

Serves 8

Milligan's Mysterious Morels

This is a dyno recipe that my mom uses for this great type of chowage. The proof is in the fact that my brother, who doesn't like mushrooms, never hesitates to eat them when prepared like this. Of course, the reason this recipe is so mysterious is that morels are very difficult to find, and we never were sure if we were going to be successful at finding morels when we went hunting for them. There is only a short period of time during the spring when morels are even available, and one has to have perfect timing. The other thing is that some years are better than others for harvesting mushrooms. But, most important, a good location for harvesting mushrooms is a big secret, and that location will remain a secret. We have our spot for finding mushrooms and all I can say is, "It's in Idaho!!"
A word about things in nature: I am very grateful that my parents raised us in an area where we learned an appreciation for the things in nature. We hiked to high mountain lakes to earn trout for dinner. We hoed row after row in the garden to enjoy wonderfully homegrown vegetables. We raised our own chickens for meat and eggs, and drank the best water in the world. Hunting and eating these mushrooms is just an extension of our appreciation.
Make it yours, if you can. —P.S.

1–2 pounds morel mushrooms
2 eggs
10 soda crackers
2 tablespoons butter

Clean mushrooms, and cut each one in half lengthwise. Drain on paper towels.

Place the eggs in a small bowl, and beat lightly.

Crush the soda crackers as finely as possible. (We always place them in a plastic bag and crush them with a rolling pin.) You can substitute $1/2$ cup of flour if you prefer.

Melt the butter in a medium skillet. Dip the mushrooms in the eggs first, then roll them in the cracker crumbs and place them in the skillet. Sauté on both sides over medium heat until golden brown and serve immediately.

Serves 6

Picabo Street

More than any other famous Idaho prodigy, Olympic silver medalist and World Cup downhill champion Picabo Street is admired by those in her hometown of Triumph. In Picabo, they see the best of what this small village, located below the peaks of the Pioneer Mountains, has to offer. Like the surrounding forest, she is wild and free. And like its people, she is open and honest with a pioneer intelligence, strength, and fearlessness. Picabo is powerful enough to survive crashes on ice-hard downhill courses at speeds of more than 80 miles per hour. Only in her twenties, Picabo is still on her way up.

Loretta Swit

Everyone recognizes Loretta Swit as M*A*S*H's Major Margaret Houlihan, who strictly adhered to regulation except when it came to Major Frank Burns. Her quick-witted talent earned her several Emmys for the role. Fewer people know of her lifelong commitment to animals. She was named Woman of the Year by the Animal Protection Institute of America and the International Fund for Animal Welfare. She founded and is president of the Eden Survive-All Project, a nonprofit group benefiting wildlife. A sportswoman at heart, Swit enjoys scuba diving and is an accomplished equestrian, competing frequently in the hunt seat and jumping divisions.

Hot Lips' Potato Puffs

These savory, lowfat morsels make a flavorful side dish, or add a dollop of sour cream to bite-sized piping hot puffs and pass them as hors d'oeuvres.

3 large baking potatoes
¼ cup skimmed evaporated milk
¼ teaspoon onion powder
⅛ teaspoon dried dill, or more to taste
salt and pepper to taste
3 egg whites

Preheat oven to 350°. Lightly grease a baking sheet, or spray it with non-stick coating.

Peel and cube potatoes, add water to cover, and boil until tender, 20–30 minutes. Drain the potatoes and mash them in a large mixing bowl. Stir in milk, onion powder, and dill, and combine well. Add salt and pepper to taste.

Using an electric mixer, beat egg whites in a small bowl until stiff peaks form. Gently fold the egg whites into the potato mixture.

Using a large spoon, scoop 2- or 3-inch rounds of potato mixture onto the baking sheet. Bake, uncovered, for 20–30 minutes, or until puffs are golden. Transfer the hot puffs to a serving platter, and serve at once.

Serves 6–8 as hors d'oeuvres, 4–6 as a side dish

Liz's Spicy Chicken

The aroma of the Indian spices in Liz's poultry rub entice diners to the table in anticipation of a meal that is wildly flavorful, yet lowfat.

2–3 pounds chicken, cut into serving pieces,
skinned, rinsed, and patted dry

2 teaspoons curry powder
1 teaspoon cumin
1/2 teaspoon ground ginger
1/2 teaspoon turmeric
1 small onion, finely chopped
1 small clove garlic, crushed
1 teaspoon grated fresh ginger

In a bowl large enough to hold the chicken, stir together the dry ingredients. Add the onion, garlic, and fresh ginger, and combine well. Add the chicken, and turn the pieces so they are well coated. Cover the bowl loosely, and refrigerate for at least 2 hours, preferably longer.

Prepare coals for grilling, or preheat broiler.

Place the chicken pieces over medium-hot coals. Brush with the marinade periodically, and cook until juices run clear when the meat is pricked with a fork, 15–20 minutes on each side.

If using the broiler, arrange chicken pieces in a shallow roasting pan. Broil, turning once, for approximately 30 minutes, or until done. Serve hot, or cold for a picnic.

Serves 4

With much love,
Elizabeth Taylor

Elizabeth Taylor

© Bruce Weber

Elizabeth Taylor has packed into one lifetime more glamour, more controversy, more gems, more romance, and more heart than any other woman in this century. As the founding national chairwoman of the American Foundation for AIDS Research (AmFAR), she brought AIDS out of the closet and into the ballroom, where there was money and consciousness to be raised. The Academy Award-winning Taylor lives with a Maltese fluffball named Sugar in Bel Air, California.

Ralph Thisted

When a pair of wolves wandered down from Canada in the late eighties, they were lucky or intuitive enough to have ended up on a Montana ranch owned by Ralph and Bruce Thisted. The Thisted brothers became enchanted by the wolves who dug a den in their cow pasture. The brothers, tall and lean and in their mid-sixties, have lived in the Ninemile Valley for more than fifty years. In the early eighties, almost any other rancher would have shot the predators. Instead, Ralph Thisted aimed his video camera at the wolves. Hiding in a hay loft, he spent many frigid early mornings taking rolls of shaky video. Although the wolves were eventually killed or taken captive, Ralph Thisted says wolves will always belong in the valley.

Ninemile Rhubarb Cobbler

We've cooked this cobbler at the ranch since the 1930s. Every spring we cut fresh red rhubarb from our garden and turn it into cakes, pies, and cobblers. —R.T.

2 cups diced fresh rhubarb
2 cups sugar
1 tablespoon all-purpose flour
2 tablespoons butter, melted
2 eggs, lightly beaten

Batter:
1 egg, well beaten
1/2 cup milk
1 tablespoon butter, melted
1 1/2 cups all-purpose flour
1 cup sugar
1 teaspoon baking powder

Preheat oven to 350°. Butter a 9x13-inch baking pan.

In a medium-sized bowl, mix together the rhubarb, sugar, flour, butter, and eggs. Set aside.

In a separate bowl, blend together all batter ingredients.

Spread the rhubarb mixture into the prepared pan, and pour batter on top. Bake until bubbling and golden, about 45 minutes. Cool for 20 minutes before serving. Cut into squares, and serve with ice cream or whipped cream if you like.

Serves 8–10

Ralph Thisted

Corned Beef Polynesian Style

We enjoy this roast with potatoes au gratin and a fresh green salad. —J.T.

2¹/₂ pounds fresh corned beef roast
¹/₂ cup mustard
3 tablespoons brown sugar
ginger ale

Place the corned beef in a large soup pot or Dutch oven, and add water to cover. Bring to a boil over medium heat. Reduce heat to low, cover, and simmer for 2¹/₂ hours, turning the roast every hour. Remove from water, and score on both sides.

Preheat oven to 350°. In a small bowl, mix together mustard, brown sugar, and enough ginger ale to make a smooth basting sauce.

Place roast, fat side up, on a wire rack, and place the rack over a shallow, oblong baking dish. Pour 1¹/₂–2 cups of water into the pan under the roast. Using a pastry brush, paint roast with the basting sauce, saving a little for later.

Place the roast in the oven, and bake for 45–60 minutes, basting every 15 minutes, until roast is glazed and has a deep rich color.

Transfer the roast to a platter, and cool before slicing.
Serves 2

Jim Tilmant

Jim Tilmant is chief scientist for Glacier National Park, although where wolves are concerned he is also a poet. His eloquent testimony to the wolf in the nation's most inspiring park reads: "To have heard the howl of a wolf resounding off high mountain valley walls is to have felt the soul of wilderness." In 1957, the last wolf sighted in the park was killed. But in 1985, a wolf pack moved into the North Fork Valley of the Flathead River from British Columbia, and raised a litter of pups. Now, wolves are dispersing to adjacent states from packs originating in Glacier.

Timber Wolf Alliance

The Timber Wolf Alliance is a program of the Sigurd Olson Environmental Institute of Northland College in Ashland, Wisconsin. The Alliance has been an active partner in wolf recovery efforts since 1987. Wolves in the Great Lakes area are proving that the species will repopulate if humans, their only natural enemy, allow them to do so. The song of the wolf is slowly returning to the Upper Midwest, where wolves are migrating from Minnesota into Wisconsin and most recently into Michigan's Upper Peninsula.

Superior Short Ribs

Have the butcher cut ribs into bite-sized pieces for this exquisite, yet easy-to-prepare beef entrée. Glistening green peppers and luscious tomato wedges whet the appetite while soy and ginger satisfy the taste buds.

2 tablespoons olive oil
1/4 cup soy sauce
2 cloves garlic, crushed
1 teaspoon minced fresh ginger
1/4 cup chopped onion
2 pounds boneless beef short ribs, cut into bite-sized pieces
2 green bell peppers, cut into 1-inch squares
1 tablespoon cornstarch
2 tomatoes, each cut into 8 wedges

Combine oil, soy sauce, garlic, and ginger in a large skillet. Sauté over medium heat for 1 minute. Add onion, and sauté until soft and transparent, 5–8 minutes. Add beef, cover, and cook until browned, stirring often.

Stir in green peppers, cover, and simmer until cooked through, 10 minutes.

Add 1 tablespoon of water to the cornstarch, and add a little at a time to the sauce in the skillet to thicken as desired.

Place tomato wedges on top of beef and peppers. Reduce heat, cover, and steam tomatoes for 10–15 minutes. Serve at once.

Serves 2

Lace Apples

*Warm, robustly flavored apples are bathed in sweet wines
and topped with a nutty streusel.*

2¹/₂ pounds tart cooking apples
1¹/₂ tablespoons fresh lemon juice
¹/₄ cup each of port, sweet vermouth, and sherry
1 cup all-purpose flour
1 cup sugar
1¹/₂ teaspoons cinnamon
¹/₄ teaspoon salt
²/₃ cup slivered almonds
¹/₂ cup unsalted butter, melted
³/₄ teaspoon vanilla extract
1–1¹/₂ cups unsweetened heavy whipping cream, very softly whipped

Preheat oven to 375°. Butter a shallow 1¹/₂-quart baking dish.

Peel, core, and slice apples (slices should be ¹/₂ inch at the thickest part).
Place them in a bowl and toss with the lemon juice to coat.

Pour the port, vermouth, and sherry into the prepared baking dish.
Arrange the apple slices evenly in the liquid.

Using the bowl that the apples were in, stir together the flour, sugar,
cinnamon, salt, and almonds. Combine butter and vanilla, and add to the
almond mixture. Stir with a fork until mixed and crumbly. Sprinkle evenly
over the apples.

Bake until topping is rich and golden brown, about 35–40 minutes.
Partially cool on a wire rack, then spoon onto dessert plates. Top generously
with whipped cream.

Serves 8

Norman Vaughan

Obsessive, crazy, and fanatical are
words often used to describe Norman
Vaughan. Yet those words are used
with admiration in Alaska by what
amounts to an unofficial fan club.
Each spring, just before the Iditarod
Sled Dog Race, the bumper sticker
"Norm to Nome" sprouts up on
pickups across the state. Vaughan has
entered thirteen Iditarods, and has
finished five times, the last in 1991 at
eighty-five years old. In 1982, the
legend taught mushing to Pope John
Paul II. Vaughan began his life of
adventure when he dropped out of
Harvard in 1925. A few years later, he
was in charge of the overland dog sled
thrust into the uncharted Queen Maud
Range, an effort supporting Admiral
Richard E. Byrd's expedition over the
South Pole. Vaughan returned to
Antarctica in 1994 to celebrate his
eighty-ninth birthday by being the first
to ascend Mt. Vaughan.

Bart's Chicken with Wild Mushroom Sauce

We like to serve this chicken on a bed of angel hair pasta or wild rice. It's great paired with steamed fresh asparagus, a salad of new greens, crusty bread, and a nice Chardonnay. —L.S.

4 boneless, skinless chicken breasts
$1/4$ cup fresh minced tarragon (or 3 tablespoons dried)
dry white wine
salt and white pepper to taste
4 tablespoons ($1/2$ stick) butter
$1^1/2$ cups morels, shaggy manes, chanterelles, or other fresh wild mushrooms, sliced
$3/4$ cup half-and-half (or heavy cream if your arteries can stand it)
$1/2$ cup Jack Daniel's whiskey

Wash and pat dry chicken breasts. Place them in a bowl, sprinkle with the tarragon (saving a little for garnish), and pour in enough wine to cover. Add salt and white pepper to taste, cover, and refrigerate for 3–4 hours.

In a large skillet, melt butter over medium heat, and add the chicken breasts, reserving the marinade. Brown chicken on both sides, then add the leftover marinade. Cover, and cook until done, about 15 minutes. Remove the chicken from the skillet, and keep warm. To the pan juices, add mushrooms (if using dried mushrooms, be sure to use the liquid they were soaking in), half-and-half, and Jack Daniel's. Stir to combine over medium heat, adding a little flour if sauce is too thin. Heat through.

Place chicken on pasta or rice, and cover with the sauce. Sprinkle with reserved fresh tarragon, and serve hot.

Serves 4

Onion Confit and Winter Greens Pasta

The confit can be prepared long in advance. In fact, this is about twice as much as is needed for four servings of pasta, but it does not cook well in smaller quantities. It keeps quite well for about a week and can be used for hors d'oeuvre croutons, sandwiches, and pizzas. The pasta is a perfect accompaniment to roast or grilled chicken or squab. —A.W.

Onion confit:
4 onions, thinly sliced
4 tablespoons sweet butter
salt and pepper
1 tablespoon sugar
a few sprigs fresh thyme
2 cups red wine
1/4 cup red wine vinegar
1/4 cup sherry or tarragon vinegar
cassis (optional)

1 cup chicken stock
2 bunches winter greens (chard, turnip, mustard, etc.)
salt and pepper
4 tablespoons sweet butter
fettuccine for 8

To prepare the confit: Brown the butter in a large pot, and add the onions. Season with salt and pepper to taste. Cover and cook for 5 minutes or so, until the onions begin to soften and release their juices. Sprinkle with the sugar and cook, covered, another few minutes, allowing the sugar to caramelize slightly. Add the leaves from the thyme sprigs, the red wine, the red wine vinegar, and the sherry or tarragon vinegar. A tablespoon of cassis (black currant liqueur) is a nice addition if you have it. Lower the heat to a low simmer and cook approximately 1–1 1/2 hours, until the liquid is almost gone and what remains is of a syrupy texture.

To prepare the pasta: In a large sauté pan, reduce the chicken stock gently. Wash the greens. Trim away the large stems, and cut the leaves in wide strips. Blanch them in boiling water for 1 minute or so, then add them to the stock. Season with salt and pepper. Add the butter. Cook the fettuccine and add to the greens along with approximately half the onion confit recipe. Mix all together and serve.

Serves 8

Alice Waters

© 1994 F.L. Avery

Since opening Chez Panisse in 1971, restaurateur Alice Waters has offered a five-course menu that changes daily. All the plates share one consistency: Only the freshest, locally grown produce and meats are used in simple, elegant preparations. Her menu has revolutionized the way the nation eats and has also fed Waters' own agenda. Her plan is to get people back in touch with real, not mass-produced food, and to support the organic and small farmers who take care of the land. Waters is a board member of the National Committee of Mothers and Others for Pesticide Limits.

Alice Whitelaw

Kathy Maechtle

Wildlife biologist Alice Whitelaw has tracked wolves by snowshoe far into the Idaho backcountry to places with names like Red River and Bear Valley, where a sudden snow squall can dump six feet overnight and maroon the most experienced mountain woman. Whitelaw is somewhat of a legend in wolf circles. When a treed mountain lion needed to be relocated and other biologists balked, Whitelaw climbed up the tree to tranquilize the agitated cat. When U.S. Fish and Wildlife Service honchos needed to document the presence of wolves in Central Idaho, they tracked down Whitelaw. She has worked a decade in the field, researching wolves in Minnesota and Glacier National Park, peregrine falcons in North Carolina, and wolverines throughout the Sawtooths. She lives in the log cabin she built herself in Idaho's Stanley Basin.

Bear Valley Mushroom and Barley Soup

This soup is good with any gourmet sausage if game sausage isn't available. It's just right for cold Stanley, Idaho, nights, served with crusty garlic or cheese bread. —A.W.

*¹/₂ cup uncooked barley
3 tablespoons butter, divided
¹/₂ pound (2¹/₂ cups) fresh mushrooms, sliced
¹/₄ cup diced onion
2 tablespoons all-purpose flour
1³/₄ cups half-and-half
14¹/₂-ounce can (1³/₄ cups) beef broth
2 tablespoons dry sherry
¹/₄ teaspoon dried basil
¹/₄ teaspoon white pepper, or more to taste
dash of angostura bitters or Worcestershire sauce*

Cook barley according to package directions, and set aside.

Melt 2 tablespoons of the butter in a large soup pot or Dutch oven. Add mushrooms and onion, and sauté until onion is very tender, 8–10 minutes. Remove vegetables with a slotted spoon and set aside.

Melt remaining tablespoon of butter in the same pan, and add flour while stirring well. Cook 1 minute over low heat, stirring constantly. (Be careful not to let it burn.) Slowly pour in the half-and-half and beef broth, and cook while stirring over medium heat until thick and bubbly. Add the cooked barley, mushroom mixture, and all remaining ingredients, and combine well. Simmer uncovered, stirring occasionally, for 15 minutes. Ladle into bowls, and serve at once.

Serves 4

Wild Sentry Pasta

Being a wild sentry ain't no cake walk. Wolf wrangling and working out on the front-lines where you take flak from the anti-wolf contingent builds up a big appetite. When wild sentries gather, we serve a pack rally favorite. —P.T.

2 tablespoons olive oil
4 ounces flaked smoked salmon, all bones and skin removed
6–8 shallots, finely chopped
1–2 cloves garlic, pressed
6-ounce can pitted black olives, drained
2 tablespoons capers
1 tablespoon chopped fresh basil
2–3 medium-sized tomatoes
1 pound fettuccine
freshly grated Parmesan cheese

Bring a large pot of salted water to a boil for the fettuccine.

Heat the olive oil in a large skillet. Add the salmon, shallots, garlic, olives, capers, and basil. Sauté until shallots are translucent, 5 minutes. (Meanwhile, cook the fettuccine according to package directions.) Add the tomatoes to the salmon mixture, and sauté for a few more minutes until tomatoes are just warmed through.

Drain pasta, return it to the hot pan, and toss it with the hot smoked salmon mixture. Divide pasta equally among 4 heated plates, and sprinkle with freshly grated Parmesan cheese. Serve at once, passing the peppermill and more grated Parmesan cheese if you like.

Serves 4

Wild Sentry

Craig Hjelmervik

If a picture is worth a thousand words, then the presence of a living, breathing predator is worth a thousand pictures. The Wild Sentry program brings Koani, a 100-pound gray wolf, to classrooms and communities throughout the Northern Rockies. Wildlife biologist Pat Tucker and storyteller Bruce Weide of Hamilton, Montana, combine science and the humanities into a program that features a natural history lecture, folklore, a slide show, and Koani. As an ambassador for her species, Koani helps dispel fears and misconceptions about an animal that stalks the human imagination.

Terry Tempest Williams

Terry Tempest Williams was born in 1955 and grew up within sight of the Great Salt Lake. Her books, including *Refuge* and *An Unspoken Hunger*, reflect her intimate relationship with the natural world. Williams says that she writes through biases of gender, geography, and culture. Her ideas, she says, have been shaped by the Colorado Plateau and the Great Basin, and then sorted out through the prism of her culture—and her culture is Mormon. The tenets of family and community she sees at the heart of that culture are then articulated through story.

Cocktails for the Wild

For the wolf… a recipe for staying hidden. —T.T.W.

2 cans (46-ounce each) tomato juice
46-ounce can pineapple or grapefruit juice
$^1/_3$ cup sugar
$^1/_4$ cup tomato catsup
1 teaspoon savory salt
1 teaspoon Worcestershire sauce
Tabasco sauce, salt, and pepper to taste
a little chopped cilantro

Heat and serve.

Cheers
Terry Tempest Williams

A. Wolf's Tourtière

There is nothing like a freshly baked savory pie drawn from the oven on a chilly and blustery day. Golden pastry gently covers an earthy blend of pork, vegetables, and spices.

2 large potatoes, peeled and cut in half crosswise
1 pound ground pork
1 medium onion, diced
1 teaspoon fresh sage or rosemary, minced
¼ teaspoon celery seed
¼ teaspoon ground mace
⅛ teaspoon ground nutmeg
salt to taste
freshly ground black pepper to taste
chicken broth (optional)
pastry for a 2 crust (9-inch) pie: use family recipe, frozen, or boxed pie crust mix

Place potatoes in a saucepan, add water to cover, and bring to a boil. Reduce heat, and simmer until the potatoes are tender, 20–25 minutes. Drain and mash the potatoes, and set aside.

Using a heavy pan or Dutch oven, sauté the pork, onion, herbs and spices, until pork is well browned. Add the mashed potatoes, and combine well. And enough water (and/or chicken broth) to the mixture so it stirs easily. Add salt and pepper, and bring to a simmer over low heat. Simmer, stirring occasionally for ½ hour. Let cool. (Overnight refrigeration adds more flavor.)

Preheat oven to 425°.

To prepare pie: Roll out two 10-inch rounds of pie dough. Place one round into a 9-inch pie pan. Spoon in pork mixture, and cover with remaining round of pastry. Pinch edges together, prick the top with a fork, and cut a small slit in the top to allow steam to escape. Bake for 10 minutes, then reduce heat to 350°. Bake for 30 minutes more, or until pie is golden brown.

Serves 4–6

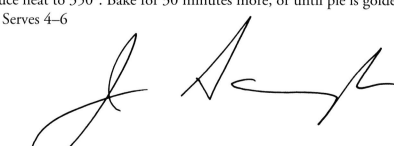

A. Wolf (alias Jon Scieszka)

You may think you know the truth about the three little pigs and the big bad wolf—but there is only one who knows the real story: Alexander T. Wolf. *The True Story of the 3 Little Pigs,* as told by Jon Scieszka, sets the record straight at last. A.Wolf was framed. Yes, he had a cold and was huffing, sneezing, and puffing. Yes, he wanted to borrow a cup of sugar from the pigs. No, he did not murder the little links. In the end, the media sensationalized the story and made up the whole Big Bad Wolf thing. Scieszka has also written the classic children stories *The Stinky Cheese Man: And Other Fairly Stupid Tales, Your Mother Was a Neanderthal,* and *Math Curse.*

Burt Wolf

Linda Sue Scott Photography

More people worldwide receive information about food and travel from a man named Wolf than any other television source. Burt Wolf is the host and author of three internationally syndicated television shows, with a combined audience of more than one hundred million people. They are taped at exotic locations around the world. Broadcast weekly, *Burt Wolf's Table* reports on the history, folklore, food, and attractions of international cities.

***A Taste for Travel with Burt Wolf* is cablecast on The Travel Channel. CNN's *What's Cooking with Burt Wolf* is a daily news report related to food.**

Hummus with Shrimp

From the Rockpool Restaurant in Sydney, Australia, comes one of Burt's favorite recipes.

6 cups cooked chickpeas, divided as below
2 tablespoons hot water
$1/8$ teaspoon ground cumin
juice of $1/2$ lemon
4 tablespoons olive oil, divided as below
1 red onion, sliced
1 clove garlic, thinly sliced
salt and freshly ground black pepper to taste
12 large shrimp, peeled and deveined

Put 4 cups of the cooked chickpeas in a food processor or blender, along with the hot water, cumin, lemon juice, and 1 tablespoon of the olive oil, and process until you have a smooth puree.

In a frying pan that has been preheated over medium heat, warm 1 tablespoon of the olive oil until just hot. Add the red onion and garlic, and cook for 2 minutes. Then add the remaining 2 cups of cooked chickpeas, and salt and pepper to taste, and cook 3 minutes more.

In a second frying pan that has been heated over medium heat, warm the remaining 2 tablespoons olive oil until it is just hot. Add the shrimp and cook for 2 minutes on each side.

Place about $1/2$ cup of the pureed chickpeas onto the center of 4 plates. Place about $1/2$ cup of the whole chickpea and red onion sauce on top of the puree. Place 3 shrimp on top of the sauce.

Serves 4

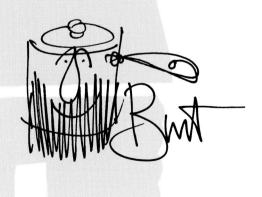

Williams Peak Empanadas

A South American meat pie that is spicy and wholesome.

Wolf Education and Research Center

the wolf education and research center

Filling:
4 tablespoons olive oil
1 onion, diced
4 cloves garlic, finely minced
1 red or green pepper, diced
1/2 pound ground meat (spicy sausage, chicken, venison, etc.)
1 tablespoon dried cilantro
1 tablespoon cumin
1 teaspoon paprika
1/2 teaspoon cayenne pepper
1 teaspoon salt
2 teaspoons pepper
3 hard-boiled eggs, chopped
1/2 cup pitted black olives, chopped

Dough:
3 cups flour
1/3 cup shortening, melted
1 cup boiling water
1 teaspoon salt

To prepare dough: In a medium mixing bowl, combine all dough ingredients together with a large fork. Knead on a well-floured surface to form a ball. Cover and let rest 8–10 minutes. Cut dough in half and roll out each half to the thickness of a quarter. (Cover other half with a towel to keep it moist until it's rolled out.) Cut dough into large rounds about 6–8 inches across, using a cereal bowl, coffee can, or stovepipe section as a guide. Refrigerate dough rounds until ready to use.

To prepare filling: Heat olive oil in a large skillet. Add the onion and garlic, and cook until tender, 5–7 minutes. Add the red or green pepper and the meat, cooking until the meat is no longer pink and is just cooked through. Stir in herbs and spices, and remove from heat. Add eggs and olives, and stir together.

Preheat oven to 375°.

To assemble: Remove dough rounds from the refrigerator. Place 2–3 tablespoons of the filling in the center of each round. Moisten edges with water, bring edges together to form half moons, and seal by pressing edges with the back of a fork. Repeat this procedure until all rounds are used.

Place empanadas on a greased baking sheet, and bake for 25 minutes, or until golden brown. Serve hot with salsa or sour cream, fresh cilantro, and cold beer.

Serves 6

The largest wolf organization in the world, the Wolf Education and Research Center has joined with the Nez Perce Tribe to establish a permanent home on the tribe's reservation for the Sawtooth Pack. The new Center, located near Winchester, Idaho, boasts a 20-acre wolf enclosure, where the wolves—Kamots, Lakota, Matsi, Motomo, and Amani—run in an environment much like their habitat in the wild. Future plans include exhibits on wolves and related endangered species, and Native American culture. WERC has also established the Wolf Recovery Action Fund, assisting in the estimated $18 million effort to recover wild wolves in Central Idaho and Yellowstone. The Fund sponsors wolf research, aerial and monitoring surveys, tracking equipment, and the wolf report hotline.

Wolf Haven International

Since its inception in 1982, Wolf Haven International has cared for more than 100 captive-born and abandoned wolves. Located on 75 densely treed acres near Tenino, Washington, Wolf Haven provides a permanent home today for nearly forty wolves. Caring for these wolves is expensive and takes thousands of hours. Each wolf eats twenty pounds of meat—rendered beef or road kill—per week. Highway and Fish & Game workers drop off the road kill at the sanctuary. Wolf Haven spends $13,000 per month on veterinary care, feed, enclosure maintenance, and other miscellaneous expenses related to sustaining the wolves. The nonprofit haven is run entirely on private donations.

Tenino Artichoke Strudel

Serve these quick-to-assemble, quick-to-disappear appetizers at your next howl-in. Your family and friends will devour these rich hors d'oeuvers, in total disregard of fat content, just like a pack of wolves after a long winter.

2 sheets puff pastry (fresh, or frozen and thawed)
1 cup shredded Monterey Jack cheese
³/4 cup mayonnaise
14-ounce jar marinated artichoke hearts, drained and chopped
4-ounce can diced green chiles, drained

Preheat oven to 400°.

Roll out the 2 sheets of puff pastry into approximately 12x15-inch rectangles.

In a medium mixing bowl, mix together the cheese and the mayonnaise. Add the artichoke hearts and chiles, and stir to combine. Spread half of this mixture evenly over one of the pastry sheets, leaving a ¹/2-inch border along the edges. Tuck ends in, and starting from the short end, roll up jelly-roll fashion. Repeat this procedure with the remaining filling and pastry.

Place strudels seam side down on a baking sheet. (For a glossy look, brush pastry with milk or egg.) Bake for 20–30 minutes, or until pastry is puffed and golden brown. Cool slightly and slice into 2-inch pieces.

Serves 20 as an appetizer

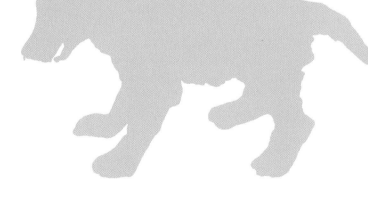

Anchorage Baked Beans

Wolf Song of Alaska's recipe is sent by Sasha Bartalsky, a local Anchorage dentist and a member of the Board of Directors of Wolf Song of Alaska. This dish is a constant favorite of their volunteers, sponsors, members, and anyone who can get these beans on a plate.

4 large onions, cut into long slices
1 cup brown sugar
1 teaspoon dried mustard
1 teaspoon salt
¹/₂ teaspoon garlic powder
¹/₂ cup vinegar
28-ounce can baked beans, drained
2 cans (16 ounces or 1 pound, each) butter beans, drained
16-ounce can (1 pound) green lima beans, drained
16-ounce can (1 pound) dark red kidney beans, drained
8 slices bacon, cooked until crisp, crumbled

Preheat oven to 350°.

Place onion slices, brown sugar, mustard, salt, garlic powder, and vinegar in a large skillet, and toss together with a wooden spoon. Cover and simmer over low heat for 20 minutes.

Combine all beans in a 3-quart casserole. Stir in the onion mixture and crumbled bacon. Bake, uncovered, for 1 hour. (Beans can also be cooked in a crock pot on low heat for 1 hour.) Leftover beans freeze well.

Serves 12

Wolf Song of Alaska

Incorporated in 1989, Wolf Song of Alaska has distinguished itself as a highly visible organization within the environmental community. The apolitical group is committed to understanding the wolf, its natural history, and its role as a symbol in folklore, myth, legend, art, and religion. The group operates a wolf exhibit in downtown Anchorage and plans to establish a 300-acre wolf sanctuary and educational center. Although wolves are endangered in the Lower 48, the population appears to be healthy in Alaska, with five thousand animals. Wolf Song of Alaska is guided by energetic Tom Talasz.

Art Wolfe

Art Wolfe is one of this country's most celebrated wildlife and nature photographers. Wolfe is also an accomplished painter and his photography demonstrates a close study of both nature and composition. Wolfe publishes frequently in such magazines as *National Geographic*, *Life*, *Esquire*, and *Audubon*. Since his first monograph, *Imagery of Art Wolfe*, he has published books on a yearly basis, including *Light on the Land*, *Bears: Their Life and Behavior*, *Penguins, Puffins & Auks*, and *In the Presence of Wolves*. Wolfe is a 1975 graduate of the University of Washington and resides in Seattle.

Grilled Tuna with Orange, Onion, and Tomato Relish

*A colorful and simple way to prepare fresh tuna.
The combination of flavors in the relish are quite wonderful,
and fare well with the moist, distinctive taste of tuna.*

*1 cup orange juice
¹/₂ cup red wine vinegar
2 tablespoons brown sugar (packed)
1 large tomato, cored, seeded, and cut into ¹/₄-inch dice
2 medium oranges, peeled and chopped
3 tablespoons finely chopped red onion
1 tablespoon chopped fresh cilantro
1¹/₂ pounds fresh tuna (swordfish, mahi mahi, or shark may be
substituted), about ³/₄ inch thick, cut into 4 equal pieces*

Oil grill, and prepare coals for grilling.

Combine orange juice, vinegar, and brown sugar in a large saucepan. Cook mixture, uncovered, at a low boil until reduced to about ¹/₃ cup (until syrupy), about 20 minutes. Stir often as mixture thickens to prevent scorching.

Meanwhile, prepare relish by combining tomato, oranges, and onion in colander or strainer and draining well. Transfer to bowl. Add cilantro and gently stir in all but 2 tablespoons of hot orange juice mixture. Set aside.

When ready to grill, rinse fish and pat dry. Brush both sides with remaining 2 tablespoons orange juice mixture. Place fish on grill over hot coals. Cook, turning once, until just cooked, 2–3 minutes per side, or 6–7 minutes total. Transfer fish to warmed serving platter, and spoon relish over top.

Serves 4

Art Wolfe

Zucchini Bread

This sweet bread is moist and light, and is nice for an afternoon tea or bridal shower. Try it toasted with a little butter or cream cheese.

3 eggs
1 cup sugar
1 cup vegetable oil
1 teaspoon vanilla
1 teaspoon cinnamon
1 teaspoon baking soda
3 cups sifted all-purpose flour
1 teaspoon salt
1 teaspoon baking powder
2 cups peeled and grated zucchini

Preheat oven to 350°. Butter two 9x5x3-inch loaf pans.

In a large mixing bowl, beat eggs until foamy. Add sugar, oil, vanilla, and sifted dry ingredients a little at a time. (The mixture will be thick.) Add the zucchini, and blend well. Pour batter into prepared pans, and bake for 1 hour. Check at 50 minutes with a toothpick to see if it comes out clean. Remove from pans when done, and cool on a rack. Serve warm or cold. May be frozen.

Makes 2 loaves

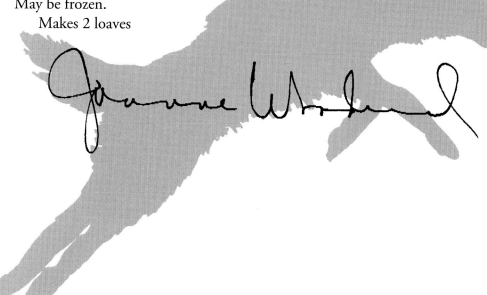

Joanne Woodward

This green-eyed beauty is married to the most famous blue eyes in the country. Joanne Woodward, or Miss Woodward, as the Georgia native prefers to be called, earned an Oscar in 1958 for the compelling lead in her third film, *The Three Faces of Eve*. Like many women of her generation, Woodward sat out, for a time, to raise three daughters from her marriage to Paul Newman. In the past ten years, Woodward has been sought for the kind of interesting roles that only a woman of her presence and talents can carry. The film *Philadelphia* highlighted those talents. Woodward is committed to charity, the arts, and ballet, which she practices daily.

Richard and Lili Fini Zanuck

Richard and Lili Fini Zanuck are Academy Award-winning producers who have a talent for finding and transforming unconventional material into box-office champions. *Cocoon* and *Driving Miss Daisy* are products of their winning collaboration. A major Hollywood player for many years, Richard produced *The Sting*, *Jaws*, and *The Verdict*. Richard first visited Sun Valley, Idaho, when he was three with his parents, Darryl and Virginia Zanuck. He remained enamored with the panavision blue sky and rust cliffs, and now Richard and Lili live there.

Miss Daisy's Endive and Walnut Salad with Raspberry Vinaigrette

A sparkling, fresh production that is sophisticated and showy.

2 carrots, peeled
2 celery stalks
salt to taste
1/2 lemon
4 heads Belgian endive
1 grapefruit, peeled and sectioned
1 cup walnuts, toasted

Raspberry vinaigrette:
1/2 cup walnut oil
3 tablespoons raspberry vinegar
salt and freshly ground pepper to taste
1/2 cup fresh raspberries, divided

To prepare the vinaigrette: In a small bowl, whisk together the walnut oil, vinegar, and 10 raspberries, mashing the raspberries slightly. Reserve remaining raspberries for the salad. Add salt and freshly ground pepper to taste. Set aside.

To prepare the salad: Cut the carrots and celery into small strips, and season with salt and a few drops of lemon. Set aside.

Rinse the endive, and separate the leaves. Arrange 2–3 leaves around the edges of 4 individual salad plates. Place 2–3 sections of grapefruit on the endive. Snip some more endive into a bowl, and add the carrots, celery, and walnuts. Toss together, then drizzle in the vinaigrette. Divide the vegetable and dressing mixture over the 4 servings of endive and grapefruit, and sprinkle with remaining raspberries.

Serves 4

outlaw wolves

Jim Dutcher

Jim Brandenburg

the "outlaw wolves" were the last wolves left after the "wolf wars," as Barry Lopez called the years between 1630 and 1942 in his book *Of Wolves and Men.* During that time, the government, encouraged by livestock associations, offered lucrative bounties for confirmed wolf kills. Hundreds of thousands of wolves were trapped, poisoned, tortured, snared, drowned, hung, and shot. The survivors, the outlaw wolves, were the most intelligent and luckiest. They also became the most wary of humans. The outlaws killed livestock because in these areas the buffalo, deer, and other game had been wiped out by settlers and hunters. It seemed, also, that the last wolves spent years evading bounty hunters and enraging ranchers.

One of the more poignant stories about an outlaw or renegade wolf concerns that Currumpaw Wolf of northern New Mexico and his mate Blanca, who were killed in 1894 by the naturalist Ernest Thompson Seton.

Seton, called in by a concerned rancher who was a friend, tried every sort of set he could devise, to no avail. Each time, the Currumpaw Wolf would dig up and spring the traps or pointedly ignore them.

One evening Seton set out to concoct the be-all-and-end-all of baits:

"Acting on the hint of an old trapper, I melted some cheese together with the kidney fat of a freshly killed heifer, stewing it in a china dish, and cutting it with a bone knife to avoid the taint of metal. When the mixture was cool, I cut it into lumps, and making a hole in the side of each lump I inserted a large dose of strychnine and cyanide, contained in a capsule that was impermeable by any odor; finally I sealed the holes with pieces of the cheese itself. During the whole process, I wore

a pair of gloves steeped in the hot blood of the heifer, and even avoided breathing on the baits. When all was ready, I put them in a raw-hide bag rubbed all over with blood, and rode forth dragging the liver and kidneys of the beef at the end of a rope. With this I made a ten mile circuit, dropping a bait at each quarter mile, and taking the utmost care, always, not to touch any with my hands."

Seton's caution and arcane science were techniques much praised by wolfers of the time. The Currumpaw Wolf, for his part, carefully gathered four of the baits in a pile and defecated on them.

The female wolf, Blanca, was finally caught in a steel trap in the spring of 1894. Seton and a companion approached the wolf on horseback. "Then followed the inevitable tragedy, the idea of which I shrank from afterward more than at the time. We threw a lasso over the neck of the doomed wolf, and strained our horses in opposite directions until the blood burst from her mouth, her eyes glazed, her limbs stiffened and then fell limp."

The dead female was taken back to the ranch. The male, abandoning all his former caution, followed her and the next day stepped into a nest of traps set around the ranch

buildings. He was chained up and left for the night but was found dead in the morning, without a wound or any sign of a struggle. Seton, deeply moved by what happened, placed his dead body in the shed next to Blanca's.

The price offered to the man who would kill the Currumpaw Wolf was one thousand dollars. Seton never says whether he took it.

—Barry Lopez, *Of Wolves and Men*

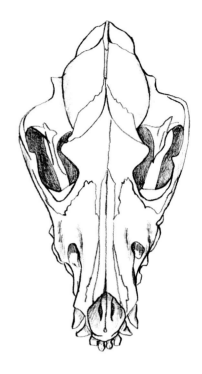

Other outlaw wolves persevered in the new, wolf-hating West of the early 1900s. Often, these wolves were the last survivors in settled areas where cattle and sheep had replaced buffalo, elk, and deer. They were a wily lot, their senses honed by run-ins with men and near captures. Many were deformed and crippled by those encounters, although the outlaw wolves were still able to elude bounty hunters for years.

Old Lefty of Burns Hole, Colorado, was trapped in 1913 but managed to escape by pulling or chewing off most of his left front foot. Old Lefty ran around on three legs for the next eight years until his death.

The Ghost Wolf roamed and wreaked havoc in Montana in the twenties and thirties. A handsome white wolf, the Ghost Wolf was shot in the hind leg and knocked down, but escaped bounty hunters by hiding in a snowdrift. Ranchers declared war on the wolf. They tried to run it down in their cars, tracked it with Russian wolfhounds, and set traps and poison bait. Meanwhile, the Ghost Wolf went on a killing rampage, ripping through cattle and sheep herds and leaving a trail of slain and mutilated livestock behind him. Finally on May 8, 1930, the old wolf was tracked by a German shepherd and an Irish terrier, specially trained to hunt wolves, and shot.

One of the most famous outlaw wolves was Three Toes of Harding County, South Dakota. He was reported to have killed $50,000 worth of stock. He was hunted for thirteen years before a government hunter finally chased him down in 1925.

The Custer Wolf outsmarted hunters for a ten-year period while it killed stock along the Wyoming-South Dakota border. Western lore has the Custer Wolf flanked by a pair of coyotes, who served as sentries and lived off the wolf's leftovers. Trackers set traps and followed the trio for six months over an area covering 2,600 square miles before they shot the coyotes and then the wolf.

We adopted the wolf, or the wolf adopted us, because the two of us are so very similar. That is very significant. Thousands of years ago, we brought a powerful, intelligent predator into our caves and our lodges, and today it sleeps at our feet. While we were learning to love the wolf that became the dog, we somehow learned to hate the wolf that stayed the wolf. I hope this will change. If we despise the wolf, we despise the true nature of the world in which we live. And our planet's health depends upon recognizing that we face the same biological constraints as the wolf and all other life.

—Jim Brandenburg, *Brother Wolf*

the wolf in the new west

Jim Dutcher

since early 1995, U.S. Fish and Wildlife Service biologists have been transplanting Canadian wolves into Yellowstone National Park and the backcountry of central Idaho. These efforts are a part of a federal plan to restore the gray wolf to its historic ranges in the Northern Rockies. The plan, which calls for a population of about 100 wolves in each area by the year 2002, has widened a rift among westerners.

The face of the American West has changed in the past ten years. People have left congested urban areas, and, with their modems and fax machines, they have found niches in the new West. With them, they also have brought new attitudes and priorities. Having seen the places they left behind ruined, the newcomers now want to protect the land and wild ways of their adopted states. In Idaho, Montana, and Wyoming, surveys indicate that those living in cities are more likely to favor the wolf than those living in farming communities.

Many residents of traditional rural communities have opposed wolf reintroduction. Ranchers and farmers worry that wolves will cross park and wilderness boundaries to kill their livestock. Wolves do occasionally prey on livestock, especially lamb and calves, although predation numbers are low. According to the U.S. Fish and Wildlife Service, Minnesota ranchers have reported losses of only a

Garrick Dutcher